Date Due

WITHDRAWN

FACES AND VOICES
OF
PAPUA NEW GUINEA

A National Family Album

FACES AND VOICES
OF
PAPUA NEW GUINEA

A National Family Album

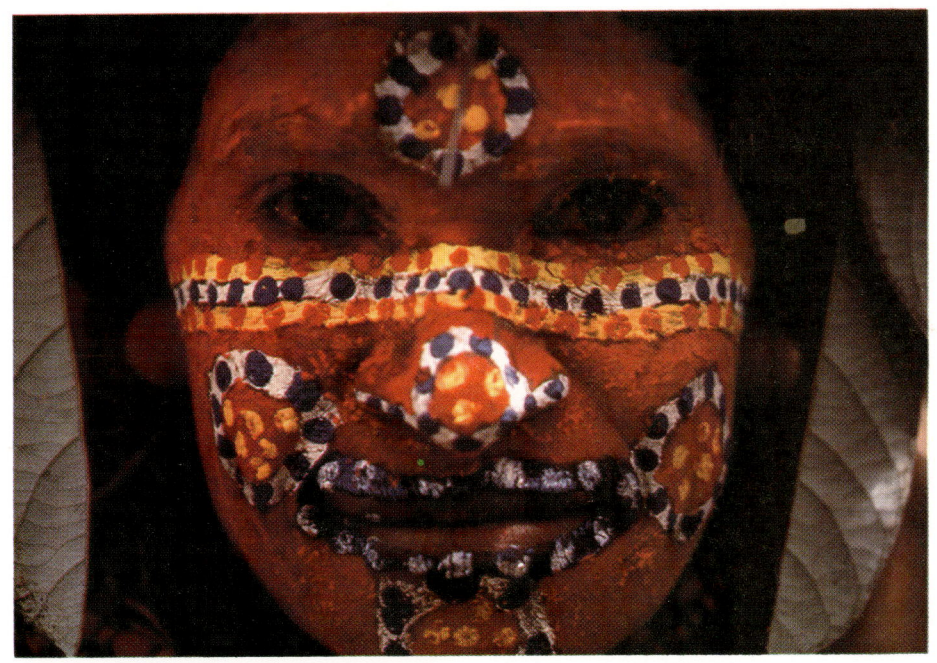

Elton Brash
José Reis
Eisuke Shimauchi

Published by Robert Brown & Associates
(Aust) Pty. Ltd.
P.O. Box 29,
Bathurst, N.S.W. 2795 Australia

First published 1986

Copyright © University of Papua New Guinea
1986

Distributed in Papua New Guinea by

Gordon & Gotch (PNG) Pty. Ltd.
P.O. Box 107,
Boroko, P.N.G.

Design by José Reis

Layout by Tony Ward

Production Co-ordinator Anthony Crawford

Typesetting by Deblaere Typesetting Pty. Ltd.

Printed in Hong Kong by Colorcraft Ltd.

National Library of Australia
Cataloguing-in-Publication data

Faces and voices of Papua New Guinea

Includes index.
ISBN 0 949267 19 8

1. Papua New Guinea — Social life and customs — Pictorial works. 2. Papuans — Portraits. 3. Papua New Guinea — Social life and customs. I. Brash, Elton. II. Reis, José. III. Shimauchi, Eisuke.

995'.022'2

All rights reserved. No part of this publication may be reproduced, stored in a retrieval system, or transmitted in any form by any means, electronic, mechanical, photocopying, recording, or otherwise, without the prior permission of the publisher.

Robert Brown & Associates

"On September 16, 1975, when we got our Independence, we were all so happy and sang all night until morning. On the same night my wife gave birth to a daughter... this little girl. We wanted to name her after that event but the word was too long so we shortened it to 'Depen'.

Independence was a big day for Papua New Guinea. Ten years have passed now and no great trouble has occurred. Development is coming slowly — not falling like rain from the sky and flooding the ground.

The way I see it, development cannot appear without side effects. Nobody wants problems but the problem is that problems come anyway, whether we like it or not."

Palai Kanai, Teacher, Morobe.

"My mother bore me in the days of tribal fighting and cannibalism. When enemies were near she would hide with me in the bush for fear of being killed and eaten. Those were tough times — crimes like stealing would be punished by death.

I grew to become one of the leaders and if we said 'let's go and work in the food gardens,' everyone went and nobody played the bighead.

But now, all the educated ones don't have any regard for our authority — they all want to be the boss. They don't want to know about garden work. Rice and tin fish from the store are all they want to know about. The ways of our ancestors carried authority and respect, but they're going.

My father-in-law taught me the rain magic. He gave me power over both the sun and the rain. If I had a child who would listen I would pass the magic on to him."

Siasu Martin, Rainmaker, New Ireland.

"I was a small child when the first white man entered the Asaro valley. When the first patrol post was established at Bena, I was a young man. We carried cargo for the *kiap* and built roads and bridges. We were paid in tobacco and shells, not money. If we didn't work properly we were beaten by the police. After the *kiap* came the missions and the teachers, and progress has followed.

I was born in Goroka and I still remain here. I am married with five children. One is matron at Goroka General Hospital, one works here as a broadcaster and one is a teacher. Two are still at school.

I farm 50 hectares of coffee and also grow vegetables — more than enough to provide for my family.

As Chairman of the Village Courts in this region I have responsibility for settling disputes and maintaining law and order but the Government should give us more support and authority."

Soso Siwi, Village Court Magistrate, Eastern Highlands.

"When I was a young boy my father told me that I must stay on the land. Now I know that he was right. I am standing on my land. I am growing my pyrethrum, potatoes and *kaukau*. I have built my house on the soil. My existence depends on the soil.

I want to tell you youth there is money in the soil. You only have to get your fingers in the soil. Do not play cards and sit around doing nothing. Do not go to Hagen in search of money.

I want to die doing something — but not to die a lazy old man.

Papua New Guinea is a unique place, particularly Enga, where food and water are free. We have our land, our language and good customs. But tribal fighting, dishonesty and theft must be stopped."

Kepas Kepkali Kemb, Pyrethrum Grower, Enga.

"Pigs were being lined up for a traditional compensation payment to be given for the murder of a young boy. A court case had previously been unable to prove guilt or arrange settlement. A compensation ceremony is the traditional way.

There was noisy excitement around the pigs. The positions of several pigs and sticks of money were repeatedly changed amidst heated discussion. The excitement and nervousness reached a peak just before the arrival of the relatives of the dead boy coming to collect the compensation. Armed police, on hand in case of trouble, sometimes contributed to the discussions or tried to calm down those involved."

"Arguments revolved around the division of the compensation payment between relatives of the murdered boy's father and those of his mother. Agreement eventually seemed to be reached on the father's side and they received their offered share. But not on the mother's side, where frustration and anger were evident..."

"They demanded more.
Suddenly there was panic and fighting. Arrows flew

and the afternoon's drizzle became heavy rain. The police threw tear gas grenades and fired shotguns into the air... the noise and smoke adding to the confusion in the fast fading light."

"The Peace and Good Order Committee had declared the area a fighting zone. So I moved in with my men, expecting trouble. We arrested quite a few who were carrying weapons but some managed to get away. We also tried to arrange peace negotiations.

The warriors use bows and arrows. This is part of the normal thing; they fight one day, then they disappear. Another day they go out and fight again in another place. As soon as they see the police they flee. We were fortunate enough to arrest a handful and now it's up to the court to decide whether they are guilty or not.

Tribal fighting usually causes a chain reaction. Maybe two people from different villages start a fight and then relatives in other villages join in and, in their

turn, relatives of the relatives may be drawn in too. So, in other words it's a chain fight and it drags on."

Steven Toully, Police Inspector, Southern Highlands.

"Before the first white men came to my area – men like Jim Taylor, the Leahy brothers and Father William Ross – I was a warrior and a *moka* leader. We fought and killed many enemies but when the white man came they stopped the fighting and showed us good ways of working and living together in peace. When I first got my *tultul* and *luluai* badges, I worked hard to earn enough money to buy the first bicycle ever seen in the Western Highlands. Other people talked about this – especially other traditional leaders like me – and they too bought bicycles. But when I saw that bicycles were becoming common I worked harder and bought the first tractor.

The other people thought that tractors were meant for white men, however when they saw mine they too bought tractors. So I went on to buy the first car and again everyone else followed me. By my example, people were competing to plant cash crops such as coffee. So these became widely grown among our people and the Province prospered.

Now, after Independence, people are going back to tribal fighting, killing each other, destroying food gardens, cash crops and burning down trade stores, all of which sets back further development.

Papua New Guinea is a good country where we are sufficient in everything we need and can enjoy our living, if we can stop fighting."

Sir Wamp Wan,
Western Highlands.

"In the 1890's, living with the Samoan and European missionaries, I learned the ABC, then reading and writing in simple English – as well as working in the house, cleaning, cooking and sewing.

All my life I have been doing Christian work helping people come to Christ. I had no formal training but I learned about caring for the sick by working with mission nurses and doctors. Helping mothers and babies is what I like best. Often I've had to deliver babies without assistance and if I saw the mother in difficulties I would pray to God to be with me to help her.

Now I just stay home. When patients want me to see them I have to wait for a car. Sometimes I have walked but I get very tired.

Independence has been alright. There are things going on; many stores have been built and new buildings."

Garoinedi Tariowai, born 1892, Milne Bay.

 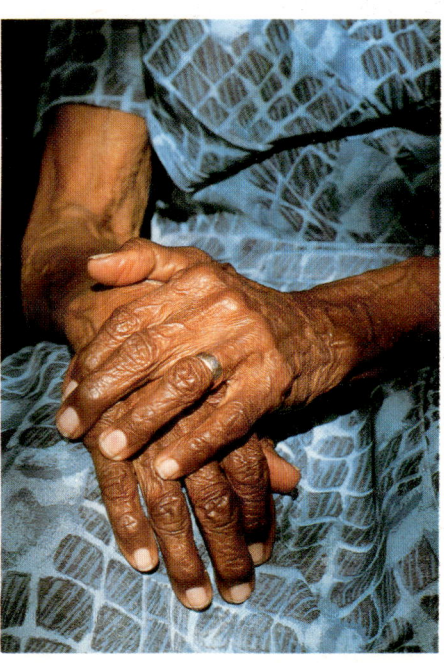

"In 1966 I was unanimously elected to the Tari Council. When I was declared the winner, the Patrol Officer told me that I had full responsibility for the area and that I must do all I could to help the community. So I asked the Patrol Officer, the Agricultural Officer and the Medical Officer what they wanted me to do. They said you must teach the people to plant coffee trees, raise pigs, chickens, ducks, and start fish ponds, market gardens and cattle projects. They also said I should teach the people to dig toilets and bury the dead underground. So I had to become a kind of Patrol Officer, Agricultural Officer and Medical Officer 'all in one'. But I succeeded in getting the people to do what I told them and they said I was white."

Bariagua Mondoli, Tawanda village Councillor, Southern Highlands.

"We have many different methods of fishing, both traditional and modern. We can use nets, lines, hooks and spears but we can also use traditional skills and magic.

When fishing close in shore, one method is for the people to form a line and advance, beating the water, so as to drive the fish ahead, encircle them and then spear or net them."

Anton Kaprau, Panatgin Village, New Ireland.

"Pigs are important in our village as a source of wealth. In order to make them grow big, we prepare a traditional medicine made from special leaves and wash our pigs with it. It is also necessary to give them good food. Coconuts and *kaukau* are the best."

Wodi Kaprau, Panatgin Village, New Ireland.

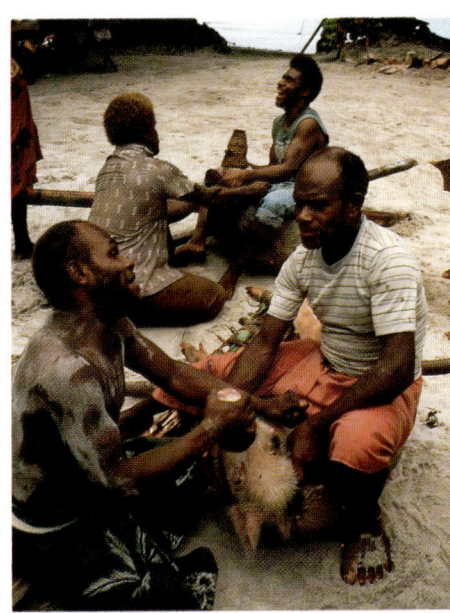

25

"Traditional beliefs are still very strong in this village. My mother is very keen on our good customs and has taught us to follow them.

Recently, one of my aunties died and we are now holding a feast in her memory. Everyone is joining in. The various members of the immediate family and more distant relatives from within and without the village each bring something according to custom. Some bring stones, some firewood, *taro,* bananas, vegetables, pigs and shell money. Preparations started months ago — even before aunty died.

The killing of pigs is a symbolic exorcism of evil spirits from the grave.

We cook the pigs with taro and vegetables in *mumu* pits and we divide and share the food very carefully according to custom so as to strengthen family relationships and fulfil our obligations to other families.

During the feast strings of shell money are carefully measured and also distributed to meet obligations and repay customary debts."

Raymond Kaprau,
Panatgin Village,
New Ireland.

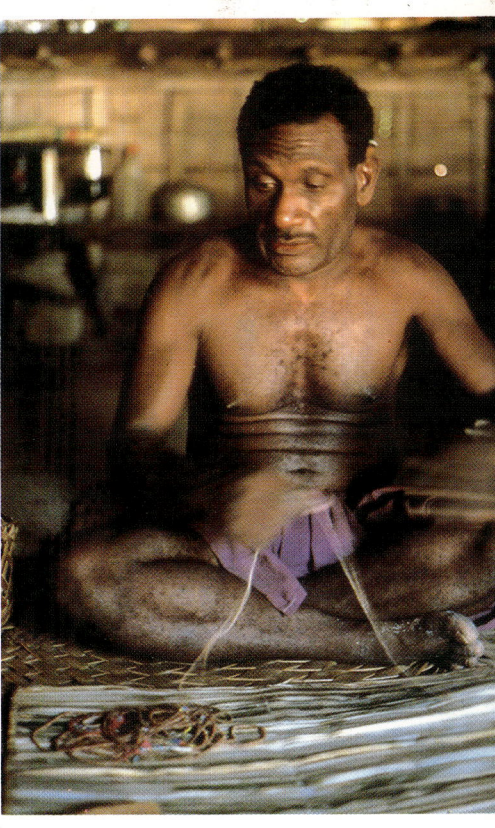

"My father enrolled me in a Lutheran school in 1951. But after five years I decided Christianity was not for me so I left. My decision was the result of my realisation that I preferred the values and customs of traditional society.

Most of my old school mates went on to become pastors and teachers with the Lutheran Church. But I followed my father's footsteps into the *moka* arena; participating in ceremonies and exchanges to establish my reputation as a big man.

What really makes a man prominent in my society is the ownership of pigs. These are valued more as a symbol of wealth than as food. Money has become very important too but pigs are still highly regarded.

I believe in not spending my wealth recklessly. Gambling and beer drinking are at the bottom of my list of priorities. You've got to be very careful if you want to be successful in life.

      Ru Kundil, Kuk Village, Western Highlands.

"When I was about sixteen, my father wanted to get rid of some troublesome pigs so he forced me into marriage with my first wife Mintil. Twenty pigs, forty kina shells, together with many other valuable shells and five steel axes made up the bulk of the bride price.

Marriage to my second wife, Berom, in 1968 involved eighteen pigs, thirty kina shells and four hundred dollars. My third marriage in 1972, to Mante involved twenty pigs, ten kina shells and two thousand dollars."

Ru Kundil.

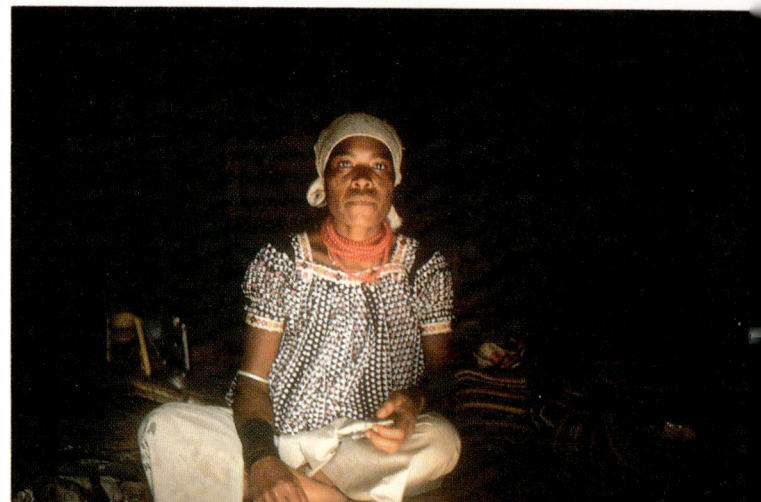

"After Papua New Guinea became independent, most young men and women left to seek a modern education and employment in cities. We, in the village, are left with only the old and the young children. But those who left home to seek a new living in cities are not all successful. Those who do well in government or business enterprises make a good living but those who fail, resort to rascalism. The latter group becomes a concern to us.

There is a lot to eat at home and the land is available to make gardens. There is opportunity to learn from the elders the traditional arts, such as canoe making or sailing, the rituals of Kula trade, the customs and traditional values of our people. My appeal is to those unemployed living in the cities to return home to us so that we can teach them the traditional way of life and values so that these can be passed on to the next generations."

Chief Nalubutau Beona, Trobriand Islands.

"There's great skill in making *tapa* cloth – selecting the right bark, beating it to the right thickness – mixing colours from charcoal and vegetable dyes.

In the old times people used palm wood to beat the bark. Now they use steel bars.

Tapa cloth is not made everyday. It's made on special occasions like weddings when there is a need for decorations.

Traditionally, different families had their own distinctive *tapa* designs, and no one would dare wear the design taken from another family or he would be ridiculed, or even required to make a feast in compensation for the infringement.

Nowadays, of course, it's all mixed up and our designs are being printed on shirts, shorts, *laplaps* and other western clothes worn by anyone. However we in the village still wear our cloth and our designs as the occasion demands."

Mac Donald Atu, Bagu Village, Oro.

"The wooden carvings our fathers and their forebears made were sacred. They were displayed in our *haus tambarans* and used in ceremonies for the worship of our ancestors and spirits. Women and uninitiated men were not allowed to see them and any who broke this taboo could be killed.

But that has all changed. Carving statues and selling them to collectors and tourists are now the means of obtaining money. Women from outside the village are allowed to look at them. In 1969 we presented a number of carvings to the University of Papua New Guinea but there they are not being properly displayed. They have not been arranged in the traditional manner nor is there a sign to indicate where they came from so people would know where carvings like those can be bought. We've told them of our concerns and if they don't attend to them quickly we will be demanding compensation."

Koni Narara and Tondu Walimini,
Yenigo Village, East Sepik.

"We have always made pots from local clay in Yabob Village. Traditionally, apart from everyday use in the village, they were included in bride price or compensation payments or they were traded with our neighbours for food and pigs' tusks.

I was a teacher in different parts of Papua New Guinea for many years and, when I retired in 1971, I returned to Yabob. Noticing that the traditional arts of pot making were disappearing quickly, I organised interested women to make pots and to sell them to tourists. Eventually we built a display and sales centre in the village, and tourists come here regularly.

Unfortunately pots made with the old methods break easily and cannot travel far. We need some advice on combining old skills and new techniques to make better pots.

Right now we have many school dropouts in the village and some are becoming involved in the pot making. I'm sure they would be interested in combining new and old methods."

Willie Ber, Yabob Village, Madang.

"In the past, fishermen exchanged what they caught with the people nearby for other types of food but now they try to sell them for money in the towns. Transportation from village to towns is still a problem because of bad roads and the high cost of vehicles. Before roads were built, we came to Port Moresby by canoe — a journey which took up to three days depending on the weather. Fast transport is needed not only to bring fish to market but to take the sick to hospital.

I was the first person in Alukuni to purchase an outboard motor. They are widely used on canoes now for fishing and visiting villages nearby. These days I am mainly involved in fishing but I am also very active in the church, conducting worship and Sunday services. The Government should allow for greater participation by the churches in running this country and solving problems. They should ensure that all normal activities cease on Sunday so that it can be treated as a holy day."

Au Gewa
Fisherman and church deacon,
Alukuni Village,
Central Province.

"After Independence I expected to see much more development in the villages, but it hasn't happened. I find it annoying when politicians visit us in our villages and make promises which they don't keep. We tell them exactly what we want but they go back to Port Moresby and forget us. This makes me wonder why we voted for them in the first place. The Government should give top priority to rural development, health, education and roads."

Au Gewa.

"I returned to my village after nineteen years in the police force. The Agriculture Department helped me to establish a cattle farm on my land. My wife and children helped me clear the bush and put up fences. As my herd grew I sold many cattle and now have sixteen. I have also bought a small boat and run a fishing business.

We have been independent for ten years and everything seems to be progressing well so far. The Government provides more financial assistance for people to start businesses. More roads and bridges have been built and more educational institutions established.

The old customs are dying out but that doesn't worry me. I am not passing on our old customs to my children. Instead I want them to receive a modern education. One of my children works with the Agriculture Department, one with Commerce Department, one is at University and two are still at school."

John Tonte, Farmer, West Sepik.

"After graduating from the *'Yangpela Didiman Institute'* I bought a female buffalo for three hundred kina and a plough for one hundred kina. Within the last few years the buffalo has given birth to three others. Four months after birth I pierce their noses so that they can be harnessed and taught to respond to commands. To make them go you say 'Ssshhh' and to make them stop, 'Waahh'.

My buffaloes are hired out at the rate of five kina an hour.

Apart from making work easier for us, the buffaloes make the vegetables grow really big — beyond normal sizes — and of course they sell fast at local markets.

At the moment I have twelve buffaloes and hope that in future, I will have enough to make a good herd."

Marame Peke, Farmer, Simbu.

"I have seen the years before the War and after the War and I have lived to see Independence. I want to thank God because he has led the Government. My opinion used to be different but now I think that we are settling down as brothers and friends. If it was in the old days, then you foreigners would not come here. The spears would have reached you first. I wish to thank God and the Government that we've got Independence and so you were able to travel freely and come and interview us."

"My life is good because God has helped me. My family and I live on the block of land that was allocated to me under the Oil Palm Scheme and we are happy. We work together as a group; wake each morning and clear the ground, or plant seeds or harvest fruit. I feel that my future wellbeing is assured because we have the farm and I have started a small store. When I am too old then, my sons will get income from the projects I have started and they will look after me."

Matane Eliakim,
Oil Palm Farmer,
West New Britain.

"Mr Porapo Sakuro and Mr Dugi Sakuro started a small cane chair manufacturing business in 1956. Now we have eight students working with two instructors making various designs of cane chairs and tables.

Getting supplies of cane is the main problem and we are forced to travel deep into the jungle by foot or canoe — sometimes up to 200 kilometres — to find cane that is suitable.

Then follows the hard work of cutting and carrying it in bundles back to the village. Everyone in the village, including women and girls, help in this work.

Preparing the cane also involves hard work. It must be dried by sun and fire, scraped with a knife, washed in kerosene, sand-papered before it is bent and fixed into shape and varnished.

"Our furniture is sold at Daru or Kiunga or to workers at the Ok Tedi mine. Prices vary from fifteen kina for a simple dining chair to forty eight kina for a double lounge chair. The business is proving to be profitable and as we in the village own it ourselves we want it to go ahead. The boys we are training are strong and hard-working and I believe we can overcome our problems and have a good future."

Asiba Imesuru and Gumoi Puki,
Cane Furniture Manufacturers,
Giringarede Village,
Western

"We have five village guest houses in the Tufi area – each of them set up without government assistance – or a *toea* of capital. My brothers, our wives and children all work together to make tourists welcome: cooking and serving food, performing traditional dances and paddling them here and there on canoes."

"There are only two ways to make money here — one by fishing and one by operating village guest houses. The soil here is not suitable for any cash crops so we've had to exploit our seas and our beautiful scenery.

The Musa River cuts us off from Popondetta and we're so far away from Port Moresby by air that tourists find it hard to get here.

Some of the tourists come from Australia, New Zealand, England or America and some write letters to say how much they enjoyed staying here. They seem to enjoy staying in the sago leaf houses and swimming amongst the coral."

McKenzie Kamoa, Guest House Proprietor, Oro.

"A lady called Andree Millar sent a letter saying she wanted some Enga flowers so I sent youths out to look for them. They gathered around four hundred orchids from the nearby forests and I sent a message to Mrs Millar to come and get them. She bought a hundred of the best and we wanted to throw the rest away but she got cross and made us take them back into the forest and helped us replace them in the trees where they'd come from. We told her 'You are crazy'! Nature plants them, not people! But as she was replacing them she was amazed to see the great variety of orchids including a new one which she named *Dendrobium Engae.* So she told us to build a shelter for her and other botanists to use when they came to study. She kept coming back with more experts and they paid us quite well to look after them: twenty kina per head. Mind you it was very hard bringing up water from the creek six hundred feet below. Eventually we were able to get a loan and build this lodge which is used by tourists as well as botanists."

Peter Peraki,
Orchid Lodge Proprietor,
Enga.

"No fencing or buildings are required as for cattle or poultry projects. All a butterfly farmer has to do is grow the proper vines and introduce pupae which hatch and start multiplying.

The price for which the butterflies of Papua New Guinea can be sold varies; a Birdwing may fetch from two to ten kina while an Alexandria, which is the world's largest butterfly and a protected species, may fetch up to eight thousand kina on the black market. I am worried about the Alexandria because its habitat, the Kumusi forest, is being gradually destroyed by a logging company.

Butterfly farming can prevent the extinction of rare species. Although seven such species are now protected by law they are still vulnerable to unscrupulous collectors. If the Government were to issue us a licence we could hatch them, return some to their natural habitat and sell the others.

However, we still have plenty to do with the other varieties. We have been teaching village people how to farm them and we act as their agents."

Kaypsolin Raipo, Butterfly Farmer, Bulolo, Morobe.

"When the War ended in 1945, word went around that there was work on the Wau goldfields, so I came here and worked for the Koranga Gold Sluicing Company. The management noticed my reliability and promoted me to become the first national supervisor responsible for maintaining the supply of water to the sluices. The Company ceased operations in 1968 at which time I obtained a sub-lease on a large portion of their head lease. I have been working that sub-lease since then. Thirteen per cent of what I earn goes to the Company and the rest goes to pay wages, expenses and taxes. There's not much left for me.

With machines the work would be easier and gold recovery more efficient than with the hand tools I use. As I don't own the land and as I am self employed, I feel insecure. The Government should assist us with loans or reduce taxes so that we small-scale miners can become better established."

Jacob Nirab, Gold Miner, Wau.

"I started off panning alone then bought tools and employed four men to assist me. Eventually I bought two machines from Queensland and the Government gave me an engine to turn them. It wasn't long before I bought my own and gave theirs back. So I started a little gold mine and made a lot of money.

My mine expanded and I employed many more workers and set up other businesses: a shop, a restaurant, a hostel and a farm. Unfortunately, some white men came with their flattery and persuaded me to employ them to help me run my business—they drained me out and, before I knew it, I was already bankrupt and my businesses were broken down. When I worked by myself I just did things my way and learned by experience. Not being able to read or use arithmetic I found it difficult to understand big business practices. Now I'm just continuing with my simple prospecting, while at the same time tending gardens and keeping a few chickens and pigs. I'll be happy to live this way till I die.

Those who grow things like coffee or tea can get loans because the plants are there as proof that produce will follow. Whereas mining offers no guarantee that gold will be obtained and loans repaid. The Government that refuses to give us loans, is always expecting us to pay tax."

Omas Genora, Gold Miner, Wau.

"Milne Bay Province depends so much on sea transport to keep the coastal and island villages in touch with each other and the mainland. The demand is there — small copra carrying boats for the villages, larger ones for the traders and classy boats for the tourists. Papua New Guinea shouldn't be importing steel boats from overseas when wooden ones can be made here. We've got the high quality timber — if only the local sawmill can be better organised — and we've got the skills.

"I was trained in boat building at Kwato Mission Technical School by a skilful local instructor, Joe Lebasi, and I was awarded my certificate in 1968. Since then I and my colleagues have built eleven boats here in the village. The first was a 24- foot workboat *Ega Babana* which means *No Support* in the Tawala language — meaning that we did it ourselves. Since then I have built vessels up to 60 feet long. This one is being built for Tropical Diving Adventures and will be used for tourists and scuba divers."

Holika Inoke, Boatbuilder, Milne Bay.

"I started making ice blocks in Manus and then came to Madang because it's bigger.
On a good day I earn up to one hundred and fifty kina. The business requires constant work — if you waste time you won't earn money. If you work every day you earn money every day. I plan to keep going... I've ordered some new equipment from Auckland and Singapore. My long-term objective is to buy a house or flat and rent it out."

Thomas Billy, Ice Block Maker, Madang.

"I have been disabled since birth; unable to cope with heavy labour or gardening.

In 1975, with the help of my brothers and sisters, I opened a store selling trade goods, then expanded to also sell clothes and petrol. We started with only one hundred kina and used half to buy aluminium for the roof and half to buy stock for the store. Everything has to be bought in Nihon Island by boat or canoe from Lorengau.

I am married with two daughters aged three and a half years and three months."

John Bolemark, Storekeeper, Nihon Island, Manus.

"I started my small business in 1978. This was after a woman taught us how to bake scones and buns.

She urged us to go back home and try to do something constructive and worthwhile with what she had taught. I guess that's what fired me up.

At present I bake approximately one thousand buns and scones a day. Most of these are sold to a store, a few miles away, and some are sold to another woman, who also runs a store, much nearer to the local market. And of course some are sold straight from the kitchen.

I should want my business to expand but my main concern and problem at the moment is land. I need land.

As you can see I also need some sort of a new stove to replace my old forty-four gallon drums.

Talking about Independence, I can say that I have noticed a lot of change and heard a lot too.

One thing that I am not too happy about is the fact that men are still looking down on women.

"Men still hold the traditional belief that women are inferior and even Independence doesn't seem to have changed this thinking at all."

Ikun Austrai, Scone Maker, Manus.

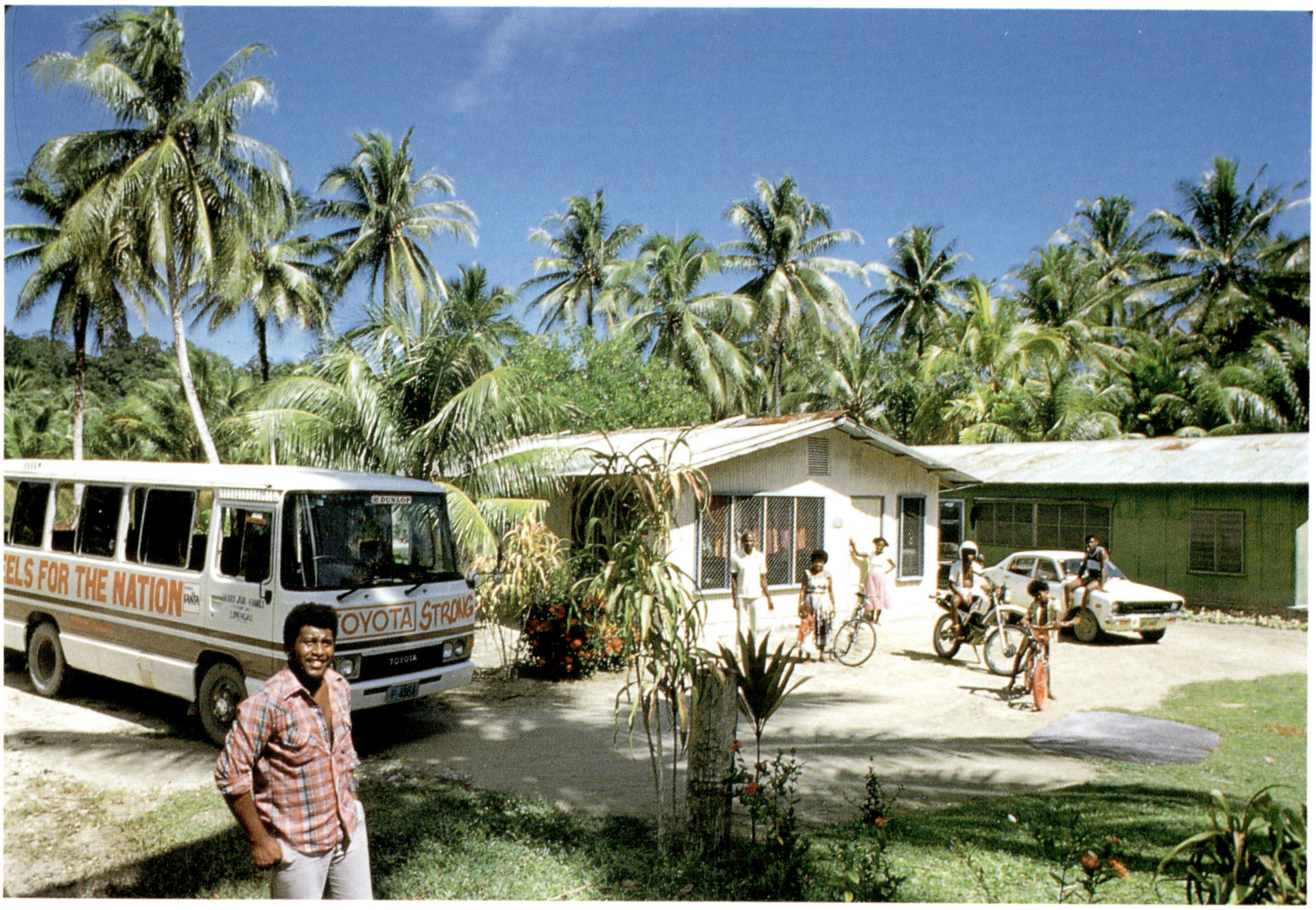

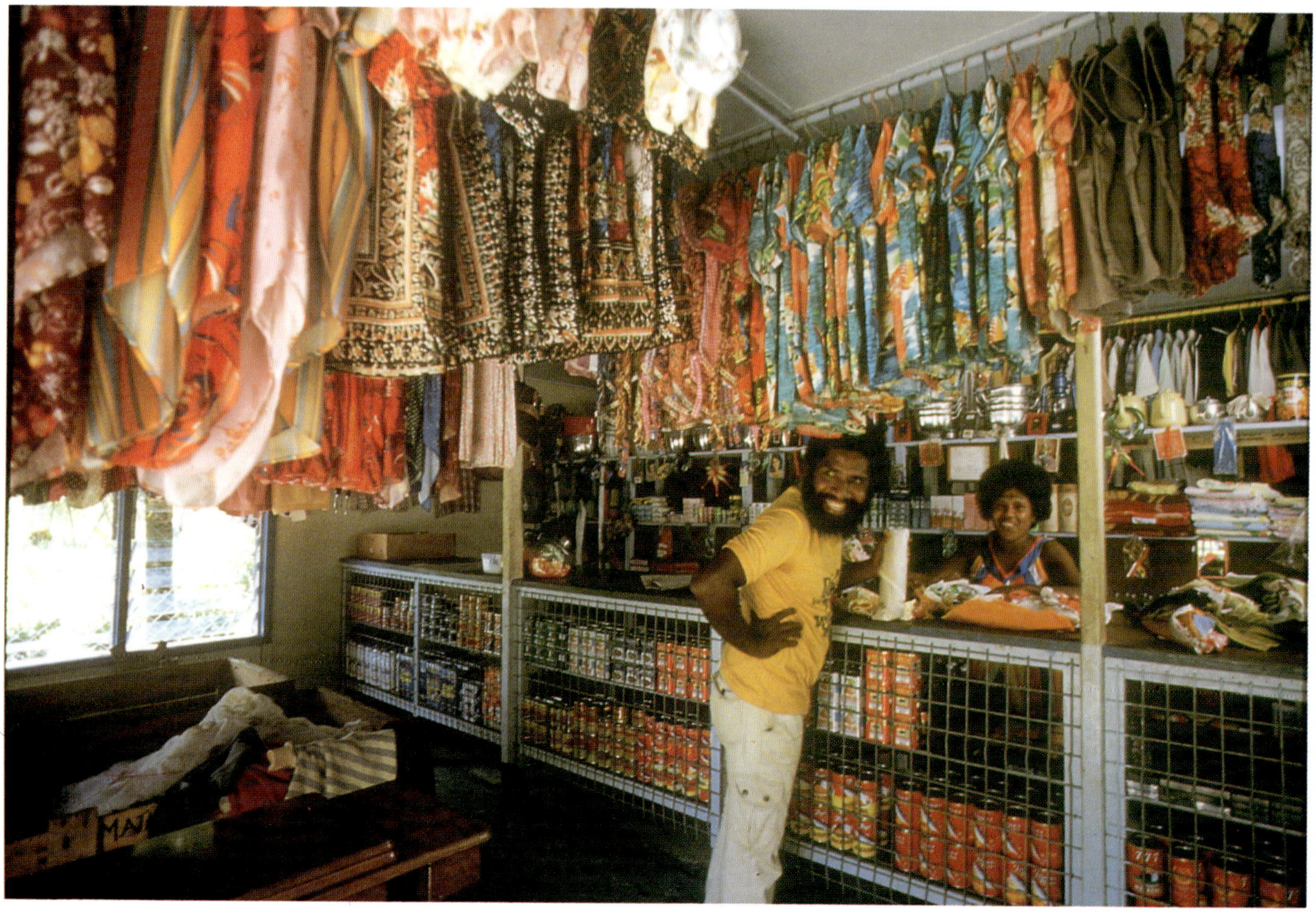

"I am now forty-two years old. I have four children and a husband who once worked for the navy. He used to be paid something like thirty kina a month; very hard to live on. But we managed to save some of his wages over many years and we sold some copra until we had six hundred kina.

I first started a trade store and then sold secondhand clothes. Now I also have a twenty-five seater bus which my elder son drives – it's the only one of its kind in the Province.

My second son usually drives my private car. My two elder sons both have motor bikes which I bought for them at their insistence. I also sponsor the rugby team in which they play and they and their team mates wear my name on their jerseys.

When I first started to earn a lot of money I became tense and anxious. But now I know what it means to be a child of God. I am happy and on many occasions I have seen Him answer my prayers."

Mary Jua, Businesswoman, Manus.

"For ten years I worked as an apprentice and a tradesman with various printing companies. Then in 1980 I started my own business with only one small machine and one workman. Now I have a bigger machine and seven workmen.

The Government's Division of Industrial Development has issued a booklet called 'A Guide to National Businessmen', and I have tried to use it. But when it comes to actually trying to develop, it's not the Government which says 'Yes'; it's the banks who control the money.

It appears that many things have been going well since Independence, and a few are not going well. We're still have difficulty reconciling laws and practices that were introduced during the colonial period with our traditional laws and practices. This is causing confusion amongst the young.

"People who are older than thirty can recall colonial times; but they can also recall traditional ways, that had carried over from pre-colonial times. Our youth have only had experience with the "half-caste" laws that have followed, and are confused.

But ultimately it's individuals who matter. The development of this country will depend on the hard work of individuals. Papua New Guinea does not have to look only to big foreign companies for development. Our people can obtain expertise through training, motivation and experience."

Daniel Dalau, Printer, Madang.

"I went to the University of Papua New Guinea in 1977, passed my Foundation Year in Science and was selected to study in the Medical Faculty. At the same time I was offered the opportunity to study for a commercial pilot's licence under a Government Scholarship Scheme. It was difficult to decide, so I went home to Tari and asked my family and friends for advice. Most of the older ones wanted me to be a doctor while the younger ones wanted me to be a pilot. I still couldn't make up my mind so I said 'I'll go with whoever sends me the plane ticket first'. As it happened the Department of Civil Aviation was first so I went to Australia to start pilot training. I found myself with a group of Papua New Guineans but unfortunately, we were all sent back to Papua New Guinea after a big disagreement. But I didn't give up. I worked, saved and borrowed and was eventually able to complete my training at Bankstown, near Sydney in 1982."

"With financial assistance from a few friends I formed a company and bought a 1964 model single-engined Cessna 206 which I now fly as a licenced charter operator based in Tari. I would eventually like to buy a larger twin-engined plane but for now I'm working very hard to pay off the bank loan I got for this one.

Flying in the highlands is difficult and I am extra careful. I pay particular attention to the weather, I never overload and I keep my eyes on the fuel. I try to make passengers feel comfortable by avoiding bad weather and turbulence. Also I fly a bit higher than is required just to be on the safe side, but I must stay below 14,000 feet or my passengers will be gasping for oxygen. Already I've established a good reputation around here as someone to be trusted."

Edward Piawe, Air Charter Operator, Southern Highlands.

"As an earthmoving contractor my livelihood depends on winning public tenders for road works and trucking operations, awarded by the National or Provincial Government. If I get no contracts, my trucks lie idle and I cannot keep up loan and interest payments to the bank. When I have work I'm up at 4.30 am getting drivers and equipment ready for a 5.00 am start.

With my trucks and equipment I have helped build and improve roads into isolated areas like Gembogl, Gumine, Elimbari and Nambayufa. This Province still needs more and better roads if it is to develop but I am told there are no funds at the moment. My equipment is idle and the road network is not being improved.

The men who control the money are usually white and they get together with the black elite at beer parties and decide who gets the contracts and the loans. These seem to always go to the rich and the lower class nationals like me get left out.

I was a mission school teacher for fifteen years before going into business. I started with one bus and now run seven tipper trucks and two front-end loaders with a staff of eleven men. But the trouble is, at this stage, my expenses are greater than my income. I need another contract."

Peter Tugo, Contractor, Simbu.

"Over the years, I worked in many different parts of Papua New Guinea but I always looked forward to coming home and settling down. So when I was retrenched in 1969 I flew straight here and, with the help of my wife and children, I started a store, then a chicken farm. From chickens I went on to raise poultry, pigs and cattle. I also planted coconuts, cocoa and rubber — though, unfortunately, my rubber trees were destroyed by fire. In addition I run a passenger bus and a truck and I employ a total of 21 people."

"I thought that I'd be able to rely on more co-operation and assistance from my fellow villagers but they are conditioned by village attitudes and are reluctant to move into new ventures.

The Government must find ways to educate the villagers and help them to establish enterprises. If they did this the people would be willing to release land for joint cash cropping with the Government instead of demanding large sums of compensation for it. With development in the rural areas there would be more employment for youth. This

would prevent the drift to towns and the unemployment and crime that follows."

"Although I am satisfied with my achievements I find life very difficult, and I look forward to the return of my elder son who works for the Papua New Guinea Banking Corporation in Port Moresby. My wife and I want him to come home and run the business for us."

Toaripi Toaripi, Farmer and businessman, Malalaua, Gulf.

"My father was an enthusiastic kind of person. When the first *kiaps* arrived here he got close to them; became their messenger boy and got a reputation for being able to take a letter all the way to Kundiawa and be back by lunch time. He wanted us to be like a white and I admire him. He'd say, 'I've got no space for you here, why don't you get out and be like Okuk or Nilkare... do new things... lead the way'. When I left University in 1976 I came home and made a 20 hectare coffee garden for him. But he was uncomfortable when we were around helping him. He'd say 'This is my land. I know how to survive here – I don't need your help'. He was one of those proud old guys who doesn't need help."

Peter Kama Kerpi, Businessman, Simbu.

"Before I left University I went with John Kasaipwalova to Mr Kilage's house for a meal. The two of them talked and I did all the listening and one thing they said was that there was a place in the village for an educated person, a very educated person. I realised that what they were saying was true, because most people feel that once a man is educated he should leave the clan – to get out and only come back for short visits every two or three years. But I was convinced that I should stay in the immediate environment in which I grew up. So I've still got my house in Kup Village and I like to spend time there. But my business activities are not confined to Kup. I first bought a store in Kundiawa, then in Mt. Hagen and I have now built up a chain store operation with a turnover of nearly two million kina. My company has also bought shares in other businesses in Simbu and Madang.

We sponsor two rugby clubs: Tigers and Souths. This involves buying their uniforms and assisting them financially. Both of these clubs are out there playing each other today. My personal interest is more with Souths – the team in blue – as I am their patron.

Peter Kama Kerpi.

"Traditionally *'mokas'* were small-scale exchanges between families and clans. They were associated with marriage ceremonies, or dispute settlement and compensation.

Parua's mother was once part of a *moka* exchange; my fore-fathers gave her to a man called Kuri from the Tepoka clan.

But in recent times, *moka* exchanges have involved more clans from a wider area and included new exchange items. Mind you, our clan has always been ready to introduce unique presentations – for example

we would add special shells or cassowaries.
When my time came I included a Land Cruiser from Japan and a motor bike. These were the 'cream of the gifts' to Parua Kuri and his tribe. That was twelve years ago and now he claims he's ready for the return *moka*. I wonder if he will live up to the standard I have set for him.

Ongka Kaipa, Big Man, Western Highlands.

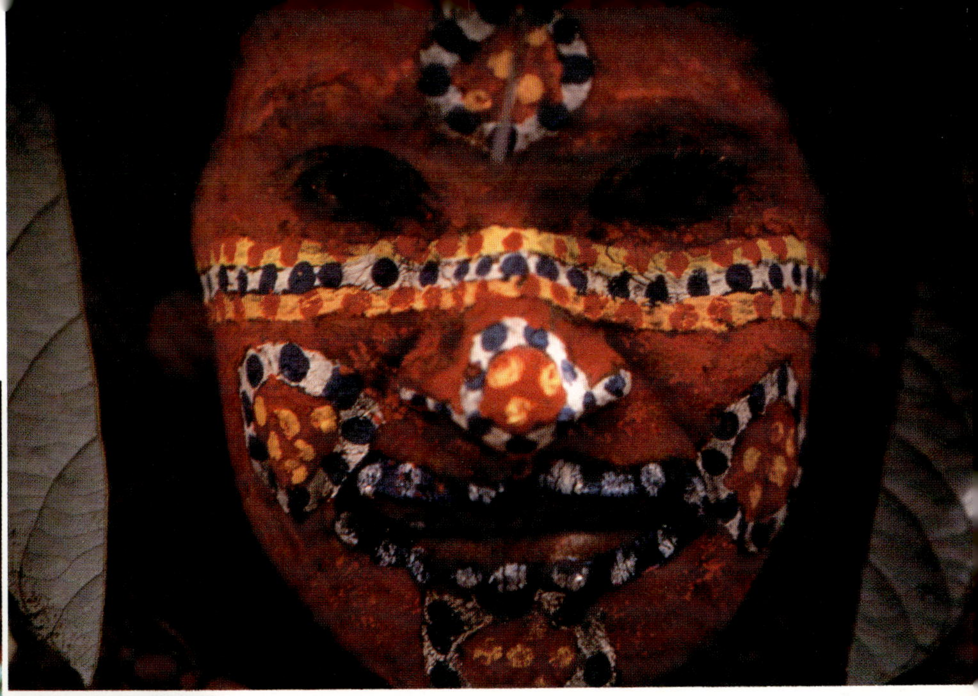

"Some years ago, a tribal war started over a dispute between the Kawelka and Tepoka tribes in which a Tepoka man called Kuna Kongri was killed.

In retaliation men from Tepoka killed a Kawelka man called Lgonts. The two tribes then decided to solve the problem through *moka* exchanges. There have subsequently been a number of these; the last one was held in 1973 at which the Kawelka gave the Tepoka a Land Cruiser and a motor bike as well as pigs, shells and cassowaries. The major recipient was Parua Kuri. Now, in 1985 this *moka* is being returned."

Ru Kundil, Big Man, Western Highlands.

"Parua Kuri and his tribe, the Tepoka, have asked us to come here to receive gifts in return for those presented at the last big *moka* in 1973. We've been waiting here for six months while they're getting the *moka* organised. I'm looking forward to receiving the gifts and taking our dance costumes and going home.

We've got a Lutheran Church-opening celebration to perform in our home village as soon as we return there.

Ken Ripa, Big Man, Western Highlands.

"The modern businessman and the traditional bigman have a lot in common. They both have to give much in order to gain prestige and wealth. A bigman's reputation in *moka* exchange is like a businessman's credit card."

Ru Kundil, Big Man, Western Highlands.

"I have never attended school of any kind but I know almost everything there is to know about running a successful coffee plantation and a coffee processing factory. My knowledge was gained by working very closely with an Australian coffee buyer who later became a plantation owner and he gave me first hand experience in managing day to day affairs.

When we got our Independence Michael Somare introduced the National Plantation Ownership Scheme to enable Papua New Guineans to take over plantations from expatriates. When I first approached the bank for a loan to enable me to do this, they were very discouraging. But they changed their minds when they found out that I had saved two hundred and fifty thousand kina of my own while I was working as a coffee buyer. They loaned me half a million kina in 1979.

So I now own a large four hundred acre coffee plantation and a coffee factory and I've almost finished paying off the loan.

At the height of the coffee season I employ up to six hundred people to pick and process the coffee and my wages bill may be as high as twenty thousand kina a fortnight.

I have four wives and nine children — all at school and all living with me except the oldest who is at school in Australia. I sometimes visit him there.

I like to travel and I have visited the Philippines, Japan, China, Kenya, South Africa and Brazil. I've tasted coffee in all parts of the world but Papua New Guinea coffee is the best. Let's go and have a cup."

Apere Goso, Coffee Plantation Owner, Eastern Highlands.

"It all started with my suggesting to some friends that we form a business group and that we each put in one hundred kina. We all had gardens, some coffee and a few pigs at the time. Harry Gotaha was particularly enthusiastic and within three months he drew up a plan for our group's business activities. Our plans were criticised particularly by our own people who seemed ready to trust whites but not us. We went ahead anyway.

I've heard that similar groups have been formed among Papua New Guineans, in fact we're competing with some of them.

We started by buying a house and renting it, then we established a poultry project and later we bought a coffee plantation. So we have grown to own this office block which was erected at a cost of one million, four hundred thousand kina. We have also bought a bookshop, a soft-drink factory and a tyre service. We recently bought a huge truck for one hundred and eighty-four thousand kina. We have bought shares in the Pacific Helicopters Company, and we have acquired a coffee exporting company. So we have offices in Papua New Guinea and overseas.

The original group members have different individual interests but we have assisted each other right through.

When I first spoke to educated people about my ideas they thought I was joking and ridiculed me.

Today they come running to me seeking employment. Not being educated is not a handicap to me. It is not embarrassing for me to talk with the educated ones in big jobs. I've weighed their ideas and find that they are usually not better than mine, often worse."

Auwo Ketauwo, Businessman, Eastern Highlands.

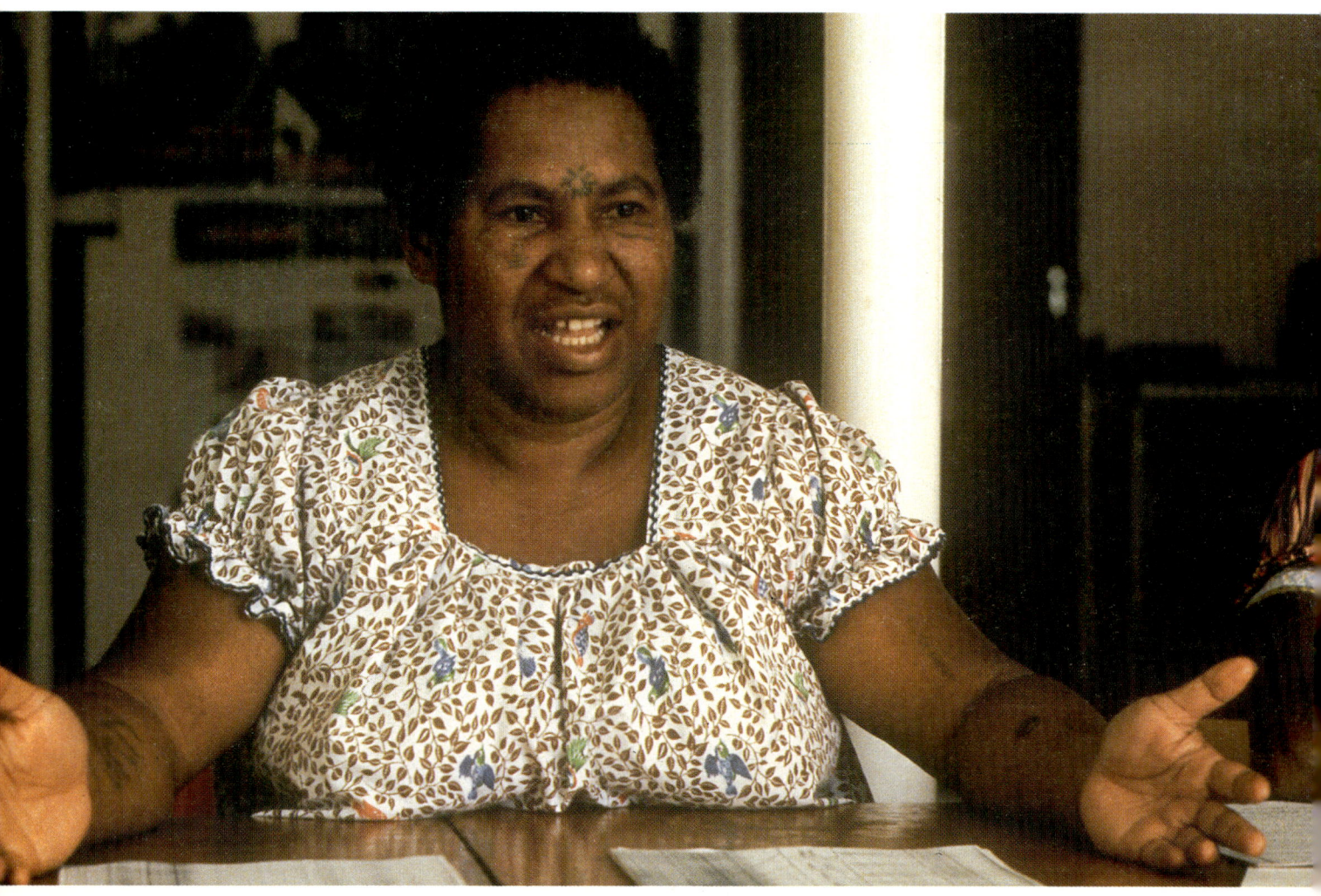

"I am thirty-seven years old and I have nine children. I left school and got married after I had finished grade eight so I've encouraged my children to get a better education than I did. I learned about family planning too late – or did I?

I first started running a small business venture when I already had six children. Nowadays I help my husband run the poultry farm and our artifacts shop. I keep my own financial records and assist my husband with his.

Some years ago, a woman sponsored by the United Nations ran a series of seminars on how women could participate in business. It was all new to me for I thought the business world was a man's world and a woman was unfit for it. But I can now see what Michael Somare means when he says that women should participate equally with men.

After the seminar a group of us had a meeting and formed the Goroka Women's Investment Group. We sold shares and set up a coffee shop at the airport as our first venture. Now we have about one hundred and fifty members.

My day starts by feeding my family and taking children to school by 7.30 am. From there I go around to check on my stores or other business ventures. After picking up my children and doing household duties I may attend a meeting with the Goroka Women's Investment Group. I regularly teach evening classes for women who want to learn to read and write.

At weekends I sell food at the market and watch sport. I even manage to play soccer in one women's team called 'Murak'."

Betty Ketauwo, Businesswoman, Eastern Highlands.

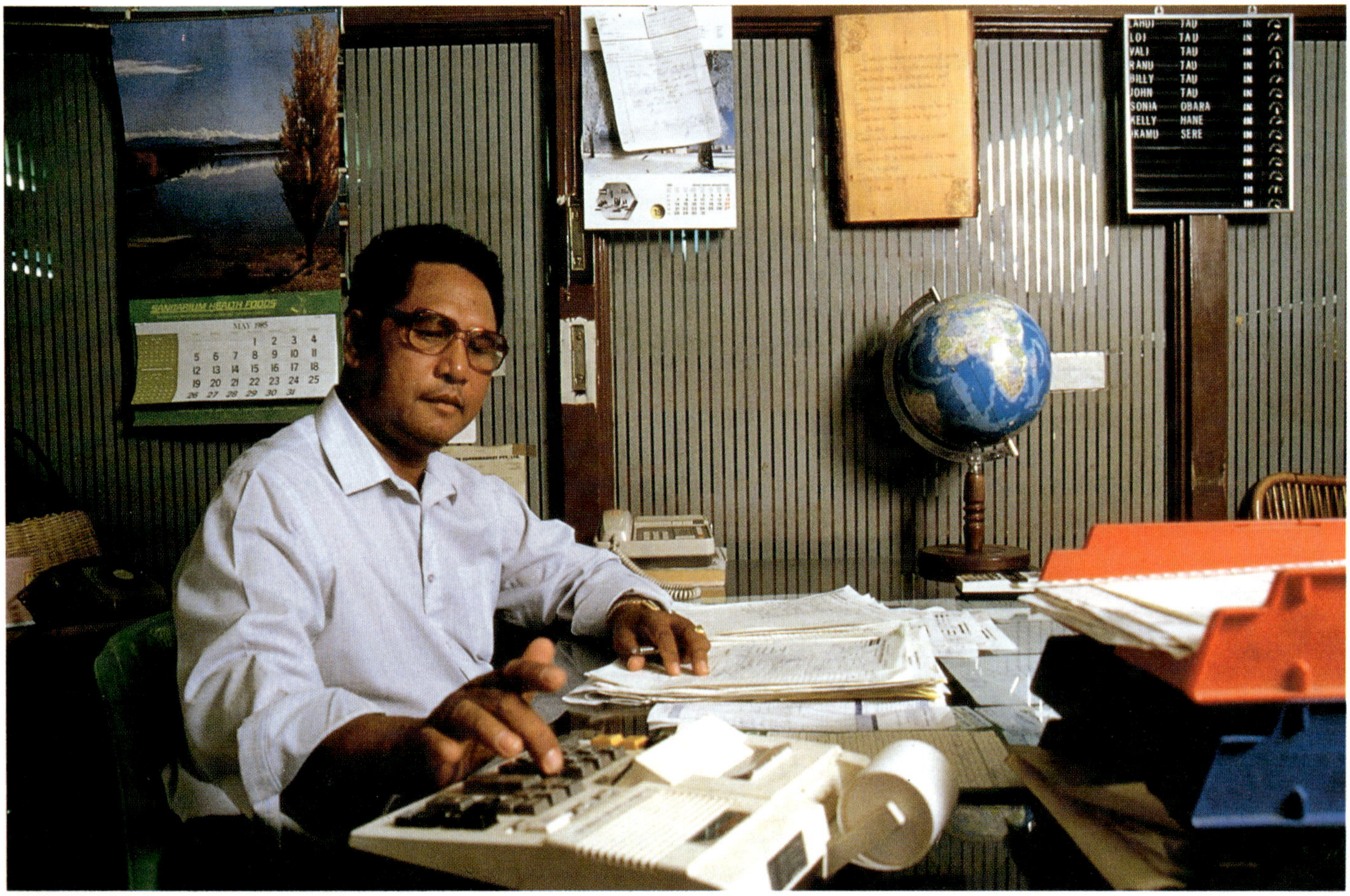
SANITARIUM HEALTH FOODS
MAY 1985

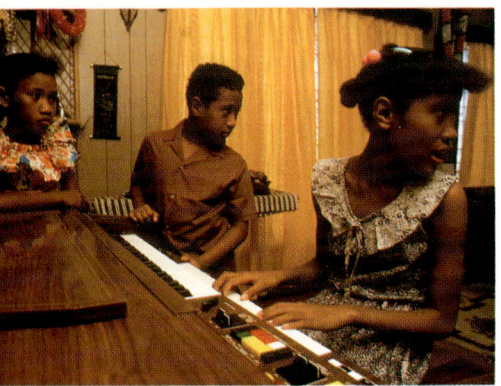

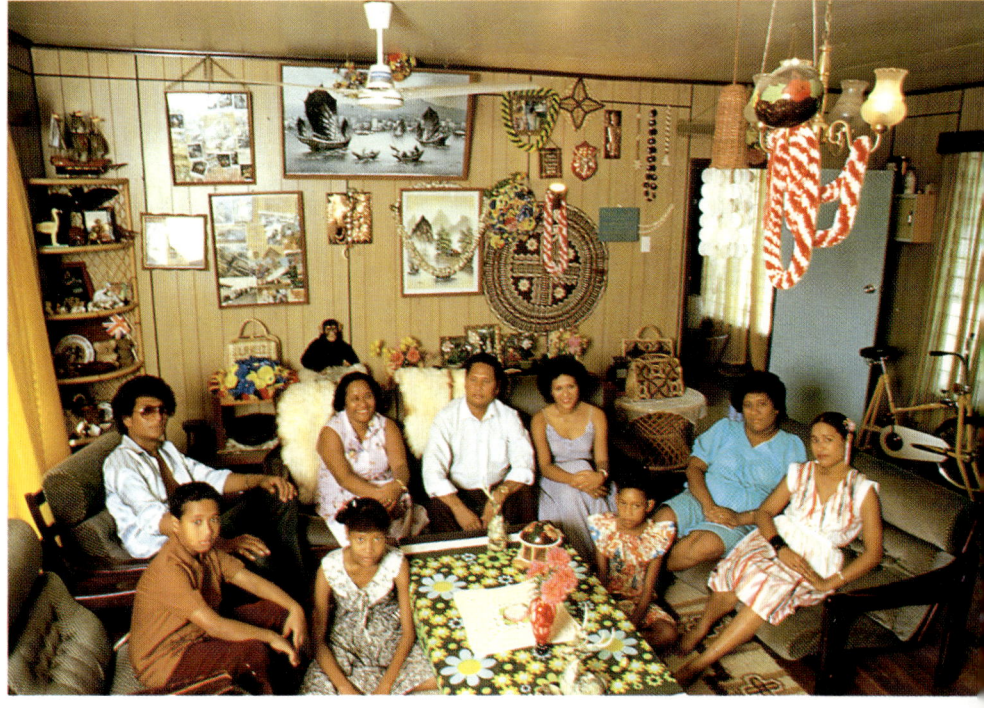

"I work long hours and often feel very tired by the end of the day, but before I go to bed I plan my movements for the following day and decide what duties to delegate to my staff.

A supermarket is not simply a large trade store; there's more to it, including direct dealings with overseas suppliers. My family assists me and we have frequent 'round table conferences'.

After a long career as a public servant I obtained a loan of a quarter of a million kina in 1976 to buy Gerehu Supermarket. I managed to pay this off within seven years — three years ahead of schedule. Last year I was selected as Businessman of the Year by the Port Moresby Chamber of Commerce. The award was based on my record in entrepreneurship, in upholding the principles of the Chamber of Commerce, in providing increased employment opportunities and in showing a capacity to expand.

I used to work seven days a week but now the loan is paid off I take Sundays off for Church or for relaxing with my family.

I have great confidence in the ability of Papua New Guineans. There are many who could succeed if given the opportunity. People criticise the *wantok* system but similar problems occur in other countries too. When people come to me to ask for credit I explain to them very thoroughly that stock is money — money involved in stock — and that, if I give away stock my money too will go. Their attitudes have been inherited from the barter system. But they've got to realise we've changed from bananas to money."

Lahui Tau, Supermarket Proprietor, Port Moresby.

"We women think that Independence is for men, because they never explained to us what it means. We are still living our traditional way of life: sleeping in *kunai* houses, working in our gardens. Independence did not do anything for us."

Balume Bariagua, Munima Women's Fellowship, Southern Highlands

"I grow just enough food in my gardens to feed myself. When mushrooms and wild fruit are in season I gather them to sell at the market. But so do other people and it is impossible to make money. Perhaps I might earn five kina a year."

Wabali Aiya, Widow, Southern Highlands.

"Politicians and public servants don't come to the villages to see what we are doing and we can't afford to go to the cities to see what they're doing. They don't know about us and we don't know about them. The Government we have is not for us, the people, but for creating and filling needs of those in power and authority."

Yanabe Tawa, Munima Youth Group, Southern Highlands.

"I was born when the colonial administration established the station at Tari. I grew up and married during the colonial period.

With the opening up of this province we could earn money working on roads and buildings. But that kind of work has stopped now. So has the money.

I think this money is being used up by those who have power in top places. I hear there is a Minister for Works and a Minister for Primary Industry and a Minister for Business Development. Where are they? Why is no money available for rural areas?

My child Aliali could only go as far as Grade 6 in school and now he can't get a job because well-educated people — especially those from the coast — are getting all the jobs."

Tege Baloboe, Munima Youth Group, Southern Highlands.

"I hear that there are more opportunities to earn money in coastal areas; from copra and cocoa plantations, timber projects and wage employment. But here there are no plantations and no companies. We have plenty of land and resources but so far there is no development."

Ngini Arila, Munima Youth Group, Southern Highlands.

"I would have gone to the coast to work or join a rascal gang and cause problems but my father started this youth group and I am happy working with them."

Dindiim Ngabe,
Munima Youth Group,
Southern Highlands.

"At the main mill the bosses saw my work improving so they promoted me to take the position of Senior Supervisor. That's what I'm doing now. I have been working with the Company for about ten years now and I am qualified to handle most of the jobs in the factory. I frequently monitor steam pressure in the boiler, the drying temperatures for the kernels, the quality of the palm oil and the rate of production. If there is any mechanical fault I would know just what is not working. I am usually at the factory before 6.00 am. When the engineer comes he finds me present. The night shift leaves when we take over.

At weekends I look after my own oil palm block, clearing, harvesting and so on. But if I have no work I play soccer on Saturdays and rugby on Sundays.

Within these ten years, there has been plenty of development within the country. Our police and doctors are now holding posts formerly held by white expatriates. It's good to see the young Papua New Guineans taking over the former white man's job and it's nice to see our country being run in this way to resemble 'white' countries.

There has been little problem except we hear about tribal fighting in the highlands."

John Kali, Factory Supervisor, West New Britain.

"The Public Service which is large and very ineffective is a burden to our economy, and the private sector is expected to support it. If the Government is serious about development it should boost the private sector. More agricultural, industrial and commercial activity in the country will mean more jobs and fewer people roaming the streets. If they can be absorbed into the work force then the level of gang and rascal activity will fall. Education is useless unless there's a job at the end of the process.

Also, while it is a good thing that the Government calls for us to increase productivity, they should do more to create markets and distribution networks. Why encourage people to grow more and better potatoes if they can't sell them?

Since Independence I think localisation has been too rapid. Training should be directed at both the acquisition of technical know-how and the development of managerial responsibility. The former is easier to teach and nationals have clearly demonstrated their capacity to master the most sophisticated techniques. But not enough nationals have yet had the time and opportunity to assimilate a full sense of responsibility. We need citizens who will stay back to get the job done even when their workmates may have gone home for the day."

Joseph Herman, Personnel Officer, Ramu Sugar.

"Independence has been a big thing for us. If we had not gained it, I'm sure that the rate of progress and change would have been slower. Look at the developments that have been achieved in the last ten years — particularly in primary industry: new oil palm projects, a new sugar industry, and increased timber exports. Necessary services such as highways have been improved too. The Government has fought hard to achieve these things and we Papua New Guineans are the ones who can benefit.

I've worked for the Stetin Bay Lumber Company since 1976 and they have trained me here and in Japan, and promoted me. I now have a responsible job ensuring that our logging programme keeps up to target and our quotas are filled."

Memoi Matei, Assistant Logging Manager, West New Britain.

"This Company was established in 1975 and is as old as our Independent Government. As I look back over the last ten years I realise we have made good progress and that we have managed to fully localise our staff. I have been managing the Company since 1983.

We still rely on foreign expertise in some areas. For example we have been chartering Australian boats with their crew and fishing gear to come in and fish in Western Province waters. They have helped us keep up the supply and export of fish like barramundi.

After graduating from the University in 1977 I worked for the Department of Primary Industry as a Fisheries Research Officer. That gave me the experience and motivation to move into private enterprise and join this Company. By the way, there's no foreign investment in it at all — it's one hundred per cent owned by the people of the Western Province.

Like everybody else I have my future plans but it's really up to the Directors who employ me. If they don't think I'm good enough they will appoint a new manager and if that happens I'll look for some other opportunity in the fishing industry — perhaps get myself a boat and a licence."

Meremi Maina, Company Manager, Western Province.

"We are doing all sorts of jobs now with the arrival of the Puma Helicopters. It's a race between them and Columbia Helicopters to see who unloads the most 'payloads' in a day; so we are always on the move. Hooking the payload onto the winch is the most dangerous part. In the event of a break or a snap, those of us loading from down under are mincemeat. But even more dangerous is the loading of the Pumas. Their winch rope is much smaller and thus we very often risk our lives getting the payload hooked on."

"Our working day starts at six sharp and, with a one hour lunch break, stops well after six in the evening. Most times we work late until 8.00 o'clock, but there is no overtime. We work six to six, Sunday to Sunday, no public holidays are recognised. The only holiday one can get is when you are sick.

I have been told that gas has been found but not the black oil the company has been so desperately seeking."

Luke Yabaria, Oil Rig Worker, Southern Highlands.

"The gold mine and the mining township are on our traditional land. Until gold and copper were discovered here there was no development and we lived our own way of life.

But suddenly everything changed — forests were cut down, the bulldozers moved in, the mountains started to disappear and the rivers started to run with mud.

I have been very worried by all this. And I am wondering about the future. We do receive payments from the mining company for the land on which Tabubil is built, but that cannot replace what we have lost.

The health and education services provided by the Company are very much appreciated.

The Government has been independent for ten years but it's only the Company that is helping us. But they're bringing in too many outsiders. Why can't the Company employ the original land owners?

We don't want to be made directors and managers but we want work and opportunities for training. So far only three of our people have managed to be trained and appointed as heavy equipment operators; and that was only after a struggle."

Borok Pitalok, Traditional Landowner, Ok Tedi Mining Site.

"I am responsible for training nationals for positions of leadership and responsibility. This usually means that they are to be prepared to take over jobs held by expatriates. Over a period of eight years I have been pleased to see some of my trainees advance to become superintendents and to successfully hold other senior posts. Some have not been able to cope but some, I believe, deserve higher appointments.

Expatriates have advantages because of their exposure to industry and technology through their own culture. Working at the Panguna mine is the first opportunity most Papua New Guineans have had to explore technology and industry on a large scale, so I recognise we do have a lot to learn. But it can be very frustrating when our attempts to make a contribution are 'knocked back' simply because of the common attitude that the white man knows better than the black man."

Patrick Itta, Training Officer, North Solomons.

"I taught myself music on an old church harmonium and my interest continues because I believe music is a common language. Its melodies and symbols can be appreciated by Germans, Australians, Americans and Russians. Five nights a week I give free lessons to interested people and enjoy watching their interest and abilities grow, as mine did, like a small seed. I am particularly keen to transpose our beautiful Papua New Guinean music into the common signs and symbols that can be read and played internationally. I have been also doing some composing and arranging myself. The ritual songs of the Nasioi area, where I come from, are very rich. If people from other areas and countries want to understand us well, they should be exposed to our rituals and our songs. Music is a better medium than speech in promoting understanding of other cultures."

Patrick Itta, North Solomons.

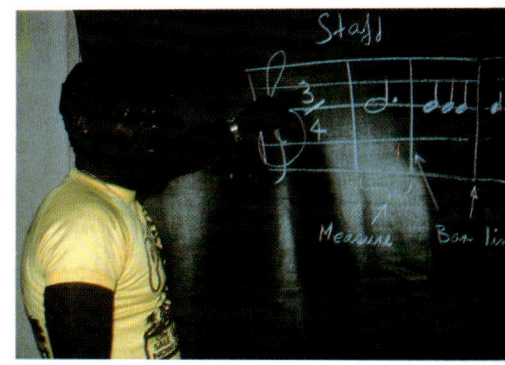

"Independence came at a time when unionism was quite new, but slowly it has developed and it is still developing.

When I worked for Bougainville Copper Limited, I was promoted fairly rapidly and was on my way to a very senior position — working under an expatriate with a view to replacing him. I gave it all up because I wanted to work full-time for the worker's union. I enjoyed union work and I thought it was more important.

So, during the last ten years, I have worked hard, not only here in Bougainville but throughout the nation, for the advancement of workers and to serve the interest of the workers. Pay rates have been increased and conditions have been improved though, of course, there is still more to be done, such as standardising the number of hours of work.

In the early days, when union funds were so short, I carried on without receiving any wages. I gave up a lot of my life and my family to build up and gain the confidence of the workers. And finally the work force saw the value of the union and they all joined. There are

now two thousand and fifteen financial members.

I believe in the freedom of association and in democratic processes. The Union keeps the workers informed about their rights — including their right to strike. If the cause is just and I know the Company is wrong, we know what to do and I know we can win."

Henry Moses, Union Leader, North Solomons.

"Anyone who sees himself as suitably fat, in a physical or financial sense, and can confidently utter a couple of words of gibberish in public seems to think that it is his right to become the next premier or national government minister. Most leaders are doing exactly what we guessed they were going to do but we preferred to believe their lies and gave them our votes. All politicians lie but the cleverer liars get the mandate.

I am paid ninety kina fortnightly which is pretty insufficient with me. You know, a large family and rent and electricity bills, food and clothing. In the stores the food stuff is very costly as it is usually trucked in all the way from Lae.

I try to earn a bit extra by putting in some overtime or when that's not possible I try to help any local car owners out by fixing whatever needs fixing during weekends.

My wife sells betelnuts and peanuts that we occasionally get from Kaiapit. We also have a small garden where we grow a bit of greens and other food crops.

This is all contributing to making our living as comfortable as possible. My family would not be able to survive with only my fortnightly earnings. If we did it would be a real miracle.

I never went to technical school and I don't have a trade certificate. But my actual ability is equal or better than that of technical graduates.

I could apply for a better paid job elsewhere, but they all want some kind of paper showing that you've gone through the education system. If I was retrenched or sacked I would have little chance of getting employed elsewhere."

Gesengu Tangii, Motor Mechanic, Southern Highlands.

"At the end of 1971, the Education Department decided to introduce an aircraft engineering course in Technical Colleges in Papua New Guinea. They sent application forms to all schools and I applied and was successful. Talair sponsored me to undergo an apprenticeship course so I spent one year followed by another four years starting from 1972. Since then I have had a lot of on-the-job training as well as special courses, some of them taken overseas. Recently I have returned from Sydney where I have been undergoing a course at the Pacific Training Centre. I have completed the practical work for this course but I must sit for an examination paper later this year.

During my spare time I like to watch sports like Aussie Rules. But I don't really have very much spare time because I am often studying for examinations. Nowadays aircraft have such complex systems and we have to know how to handle them properly.

Normally when new aircraft arrive, we undergo some theoretical and practical courses on the new model. It is the operating company's responsibility to make sure that the pilots and the maintenance personnel have the necessary training for the new planes."

Peter Kankonaru, Aircraft Engineer, Morobe.

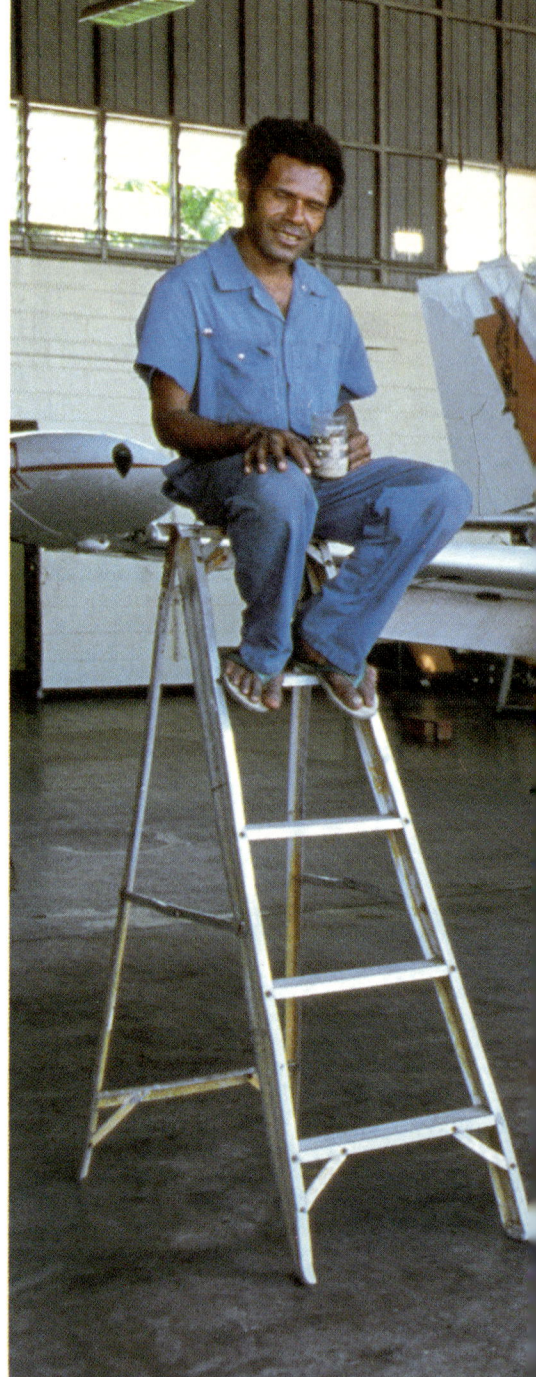

"Regarding these ten years of Independence I think that, generally, we are improving. Lots of locals are engaged in private businesses, localisation has been taking place in both the public and private sectors.

The law and order problem is occurring because I believe Papua New Guinea is adopting western culture too rapidly instead of going one step at a time."

"When westerners were undergoing their own process of civilisation the pace of changes was more gradual and they all developed together, whereas, here in Papua New Guinea we are developing more quickly and more unevenly. And we are mainly copying civilised developed countries. We should be walking but instead we have jumped from the very bottom to the top in a matter of decades. We are going through the civilisation period much faster than others."

Peter Kankonaru, Talair Aircraft Engineer, Morobe.

"A significant proportion of the population of Papua New Guinea lives near volcanoes and are subject to the risks associated with eruptions and earthquakes. Here in Rabaul we are constantly measuring seismic activity and obtaining ground deformation data.

We also monitor ground and sea temperature, ocean levels and water colour. Much of our equipment is very advanced. For example we have an instrument that emits laser beams to certain fixed locations to accurately measure any possible ground deformation and our instruments feed data into a computer which helps us analyse it.

I have had some training in Hawaii and on the US mainland, and I think this is important to keep us in touch and to draw on international expertise.

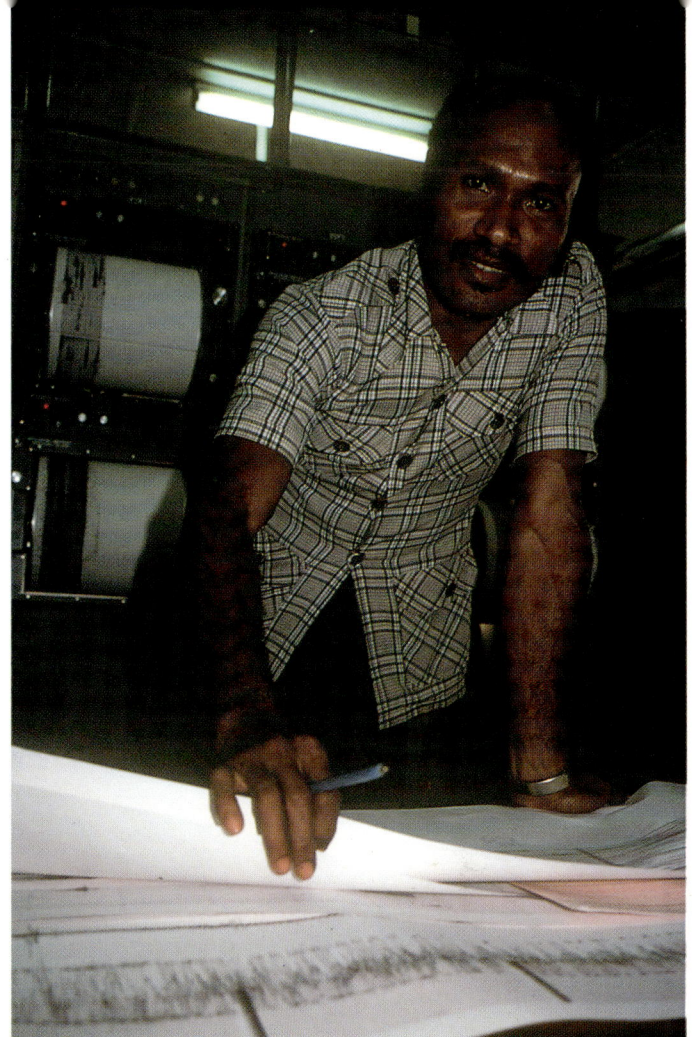

"We can't see past the ground surface and so it fascinates me to imagine what kind of turmoil is going on deep down; the data we collect can tell us a lot. If there's going to be an eruption we will be able to predict and warn the people. I don't want a repetition of the 1937 tragedy when an eruption killed two thousand people."

Benjamin Talai, Vulcanologist, East New Britain.

"It's a good thing that we gained Independence when we did, otherwise we'd probably be going through what the New Caledonians are now experiencing. It could have been worse in fact because we have a larger population and many different groups. Papua New Guinea is still a peaceful country compared with others in the world.

There should however be a national awareness campaign to help people realise the potential dangers. I have undergone training and participated in exercises in Australia, Hawaii and mainland U.S.A. and I can see the dangers of superpower rivalry and tensions in South East Asia. The possibility that Papua New Guinea could again be a battleground or a 'stepping stone' for other nations' armies should not be ignored. The public should know, however, that there is a trained group of disciplined men to call in when needed. But we need more financial and logistic support.

In 1980 when the Santo thing came up we sent a company of soldiers at the request of the Vanuatu Government and I too participated. We were successful because we were well trained and logistic support was readily available.

The army develops young men's personal discipline and maturity; teaches them what to do and what not to do. The routine discipline of army life makes good citizens.

In addition to seeing more schools opened. I would like to see some form of national service introduced for all young people. It would help solve the problem of unemployment and make better citizens."

Captain Jerry Singirok, Commanding Officer, P.I.R. Support Company, Vanimo.

"The expectations of parents for their children are very high. They hope to see them progress to Grade 6 and beyond through high school and higher education to obtain wage employment. But the educational system does not offer enough places in schools, colleges and universities while the country does not offer enough employment opportunities. So frustration and disappointment are inevitable. The children who experience some schooling learn to read and write in English and do arithmetic – concepts and skills beyond the practicality of the village. In other words the children who can't get jobs and go back to the village are useless there. So right now they're talking about gangsters and robbery and all those in towns are multiplying in number because we are not changing direction. There should be more practical activities in primary schools. Everyone should do a lot of manual work. The prime aim of education should be to enable youth to grow to be better men and women at home."

Jim Yer, Headmaster, Simbu.

"It was when I was in primary school I made up my mind to become a teacher because I was really interested in kids — working with them, playing with them. My first experience was as a Sunday School teacher and I liked that. After training at Madang Teachers' College I was posted to Kerowagi School in 1983. That's when I met Jim who was headmaster at the time and we eventually got married."

Toka Daina Yer, School Teacher, Simbu.

"I personally think that the *Viles Tok Ples Skuls* are very important. We are not training kids to go as far as university; this is not our aim. Some will go, no doubt, but our main objective is that the children do not lose their language, do not lose their culture, do not lose their traditional respect. And the culture is the essence of *Viles Tok Ples Skuls;* that children know where they belong, know their traditional wealth, whatever they have to do with this wealth, and know their land rights and everything else in their society. So, all in all, identity, belonging to a group, and a pride come out with all this in culture and language."

Ruth Saovana-Spriggs, Viles Tok Ples Skul Co-ordinator, North Solomons Province.

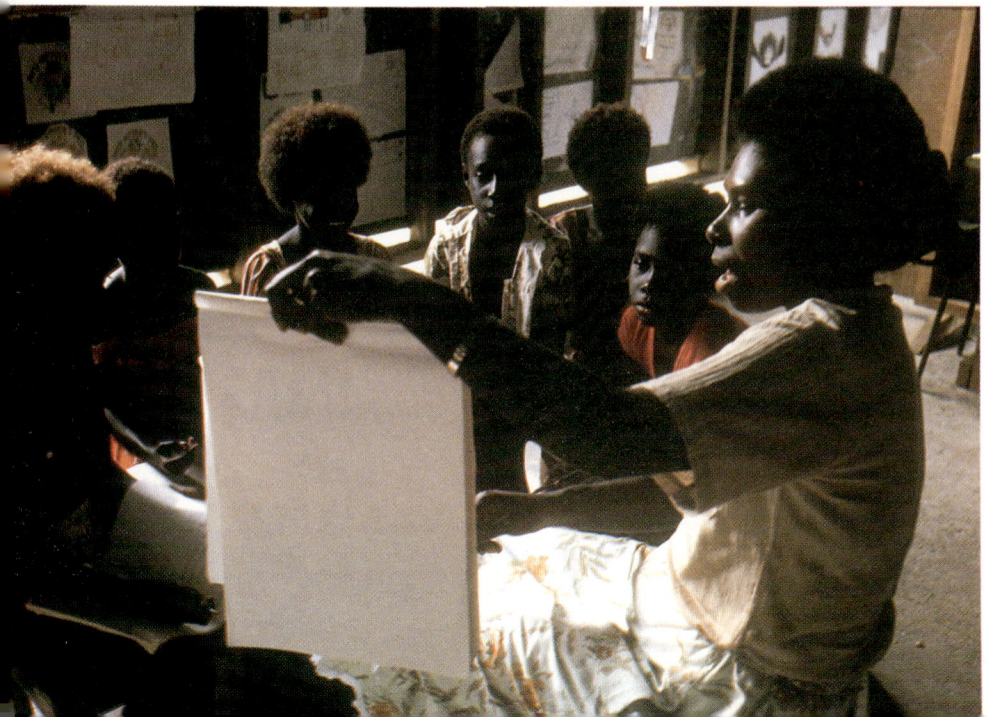

"I visit all the *Tok Ples Skuls* in the Province to see how the teachers are getting on. I help them make their own books by cutting pictures from magazines and writing stories about them in our language. We have to make our own books because we don't have enough printed in *'tok ples'*. The publication of books is still a long way off unless someone is willing to publish them for us.

On the cultural side, we invite old people to come to school and tell stories and talk about our culture. We need a tape recorder to collect these."

Rachel Kaetavara, Tok Ples Skuls Teacher, North Solomons.

"I think that children who do grades one and two in their own language have the advantage over those who start schooling in English. By being taught in their own language they start to understand things better at an early age and they have a better foundation in science and maths when they join the community school in grade three."

Aloysius Niabu, Tok Ples School Teacher, North Solomons.

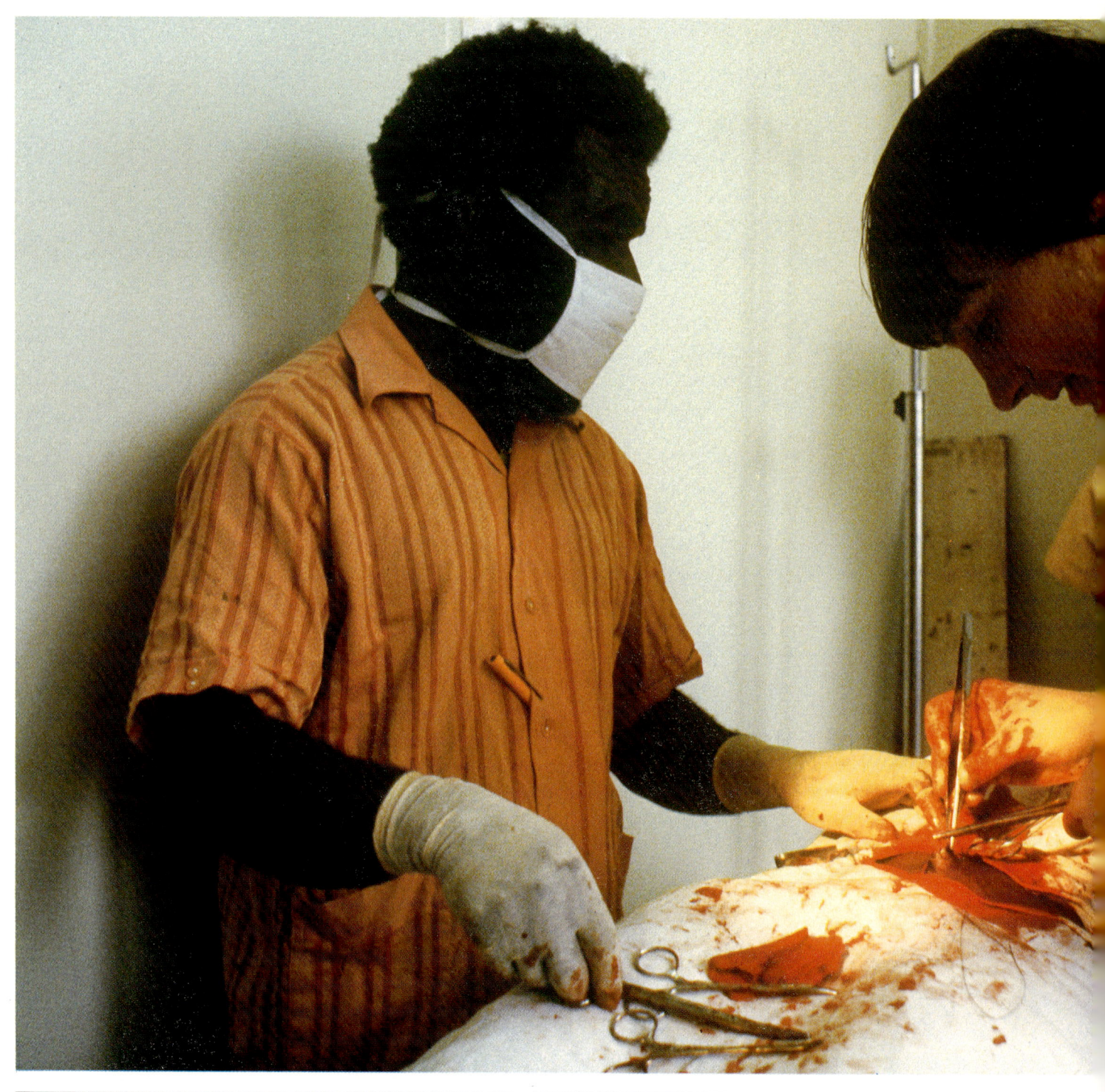

"I first joined the Department of Public Health in 1954. I have not had any schooling or formal medical training, but I have had plenty of on-the-job training. In the early days the doctors would give us *dokta bois* afternoon classes and I learned how to detect and cure many common illnesses. I know the names of many medicines and how to perform certain clinical procedures. My speciality is in the removal of splinters, bottles, arrows, spears and other foreign materials from the body. Patients often ask me to help them with a remedy for illnesses caused by sorcery but I insist that I deal only with illnesses that have a medical or physiological basis. The nature of the patients complaints is gradually changing. For example, diseases like *pig bel* and malaria have declined but, since the opening of the Highlands Highway from Mt. Hagen to Mendi and Lae, the number of car accident victims has increased.

Tari Hospital used to be no more than an aid post for outpatients. In recent years the facilities and services it offers have improved. We now have an operating theatre, a pathology laboratory, a labour ward, an X-ray machine, a dispensary and dental facilities. There are also improved kitchen and laundry facilities and I shouldn't forget to mention the newer and better morgue.

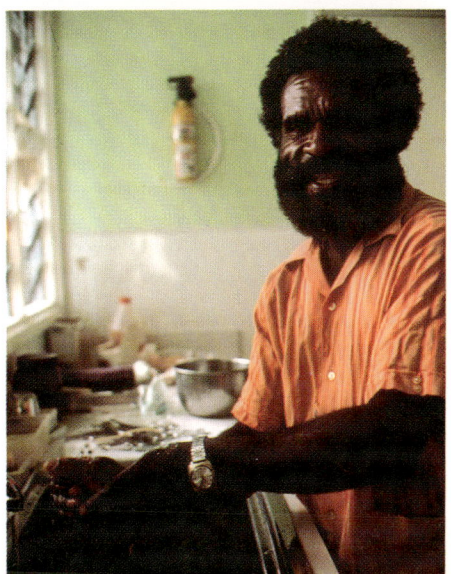

"Our big worry is the frequent shortage of qualified staff."

James Muli, Medical Orderly,
Southern Highlands.

"The women's group activities include baking in drum ovens, cooking on charcoal stoves, constructing toilets and water tanks to ensure a clean water supply. We also learn new methods of gardening. For example, we used to burn the grass before planting; now we dig it in and use it as mulch.

We stress the importance of a nutritious diet – especially for children and sick people.

As the ideas and methods are new, they are repeated and practised until they are well understood. We hope our husbands and leaders will learn from us and support our efforts."

Akapina Tonave, Nutritionist, East Sepik.

"The National Council of Women has organised workshops on book-keeping, the establishment of small scale business, management and leadership. We have worked in conjunction with various government departments like Primary Industry, Health and Commerce to organise training programs in different provinces. We have successfully pressed for the inclusion of women in higher ranking bodies like the Law Reform Commission, the Ombudsman Commission and the Public Services Commission. From our resources we have been able to provide some financial assistance to other women's organisations and we have helped arrange for voluntary workers from within and without the country to assist in the management of women's projects.

Today is a meeting of the Eastern Highlands Provincial Council and we have been working on improvements to our constitution, and on plans for the construction of a Women's Resource Centre; a major project for which we will have to raise K360,000. I reported to the meeting on a recent trip to China by a women's delegation and on my participation in the latest Pacific Islands Regional Meeting in Raratonga.

We are also working on fund raising for celebrations to mark the end of the World Decade for Women."

> Angela Soso, President,
> National Council of Women, Eastern Highlands.

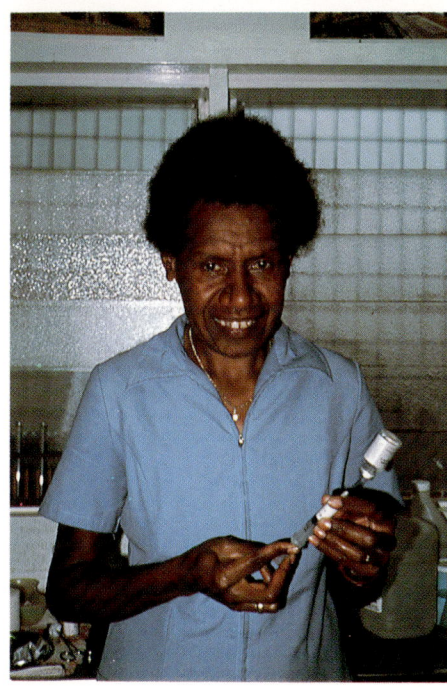

"I cannot tell you exactly what I would do in a normal day because I use a sort of 'take it as it comes' method. Many of the villagers I deal with cannot understand the importance of an appointment and don't bother to turn up at an appointed time. Some days I attend to administrative routines — correspondence, ordering supplies and so forth. Sometimes I am called to offer emergency counselling to a troubled client. I often visit homes and monitor the welfare of families and children.

As part of my duty I compile reports for the police to present in court. It is important to be a good listener so that people with problems can share their burdens. Once a frustrated father killed his own child — bashed its brains out — at the police station because he felt there was no one who could really understand his problems.

Juvenile delinquency, the adoption of children, marriage and child custody disputes are the most common matters that I attend to."

Gladys Yadiwillo, Community Welfare Officer, Eastern Highlands.

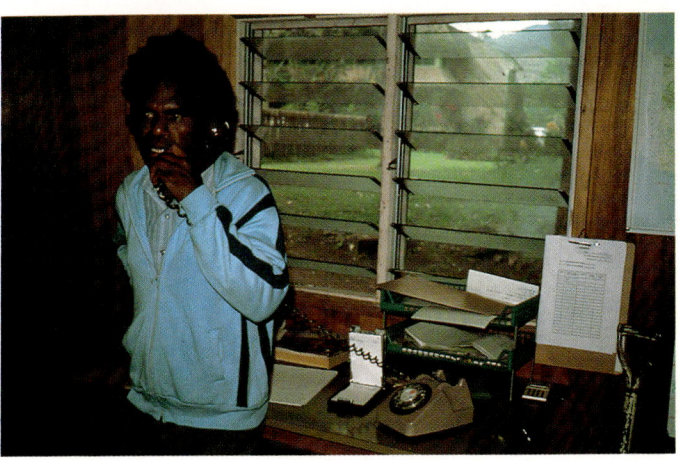

"I first became interested in working with lawbreakers when I saw the Sacred Heart Brothers running Boys' Town in Wewak. Since January 1985 I have been involved in the establishment of a probation system for juvenile offenders. German and Canadian volunteers are also involved in this project. We are keeping track of youth who have been placed on probation by the courts. We advise them, help them to find work, and encourage them to get involved in community work, agricultural or commercial projects. But our work goes further than that sometimes for we are expected to help keep law and order, to settle disputes and to help arrange compensation for people who have suffered at the hands of these youths.

Agricultural projects like the one we're working on now give the youth work and involvement with the community. I'm glad to say that the crime rate is now down in the Daulo area and I'm sure this is partly the result of our efforts."

Leo Tohichem, Probation Officer, Eastern Highlands.

"It is difficult to arrange financial assistance for youth groups to get them started and when we do the grants are usually very small. In fact, the cost of bringing a young offender to court and putting him through the court system would usually be greater than the value of the grants given to help youth groups."

Leo Tohichem.

"I am the leader of a youth group in the Daulo Pass area. We have sixty-four members and we call ourselves the Rokiku Youth Group. So many of the young people in our area couldn't find work so we gathered together and decided to form this group. The village people collected three hundred kina to help us get started.

We used this money to buy red coffee cherries from village growers. We then hulled, dried and sold them to the coffee factory for growers. We also earn money by picking coffee for growers. Now we are establishing our own coffee plantation on twenty hectares of land that the village people have marked out for us.

We won a construction contract to build a road into our village and twenty-seven members are working on that. They are donating additional voluntary labour to this contract to the value of about one thousand five hundred kina. But mainly we rely on coffee and during the off season we are short of money so we are also getting involved in other projects. We even make and sell coffins and we have started a trade store.

At present we are trying to get a bank loan to buy a video system so we can screen video tapes and charge admission."

Wanopa Kenda, Youth Leader,
Eastern Highlands.

"In the area near the Daulo Pass there used to be a lot of fighting and highway robbery. Rascal gangs would attack and rob vehicles climbing the pass and the area had a very bad reputation.

In the last three years there has been a great deal of effort to recognise and overcome the problems. We have been fortunate to have had the support of the Eastern Highlands Rehabilitation Committee – a voluntary body – and assistance from the Chief Magistrate, Rick Giddings and his wife Lynn.

The gangs have been reformed into youth groups and have been encouraged to become involved in community youth assistance projects and money-making ventures.

There's still a lot to be done but there is evidence of some success. The youth groups have been involved in road building, coffee planting and picking, and operating stores. I urge the Government to give more support to the Rehabilitation Committee."

Niki Amaia, Youth Projects Officer, Eastern Highlands.

"I come from Tapini in the Central Province and I now live in Morata. It's a good place but I can't find work and I've been trying for years. *Mi stap nating.* And all my family are with me and none of them have found work either.

There are unemployed youth all around and they are really doing bad things. We've got to find work or things are going to get worse.

How can I celebrate Independence when I'm worried about work."

Labai Toani, Unemployed, Morata.

"I came from Goroka in 1976 to work for wages and when I failed, I joined a rascal gang called '105 Waga.' I became the leader. Our activities included 'break and enter' and stealing cars. Sometimes we would operate in conjunction with other gangs like '585' and 'Bomai'. The last crime I was involved in was stealing a police car but I was caught and went to jail.

When I came out I changed my ways. I got a job with the Housing Commission and then I was appointed Chairman of the Morata Village Court.

The people who leave their villages and come to Moresby don't come to fight or steal or become 'big heads', no. They only come to look for work and when they fail they steal."

Timothy Kilami, Former Gang Leader, Morata.

"Papua New Guinea is a wonderful place but in Morata the talk is all about the 'rascals' and 'break and enter'. We are trying to help these people to be happy and live well together.

The 'rascals' are still following their ways because there is not enough employment for them and because their parents did not teach them about the love of God.

All men and women need God's love."

Sister Balbine, Catholic Sister, Morata.

"Since Independence we have gained many good things. For example near here you can see our new House of Parliament. I'm proud of that. But in the seven years since I left Tari and have lived at Morata I have noted the increasing unemployment. There are too many *pasindias*, mainly among the youth. With no school, no work and no effective government here in Morata, they become rascals and steal cars, money and goods, they attack people and spoil everything.

The police come in, chase and jail them, but it doesn't really help. We village peace officers and village court magistrates try our best to control them but what they really need is employment."

Alembo Nano, Peace Officer, National Capital.

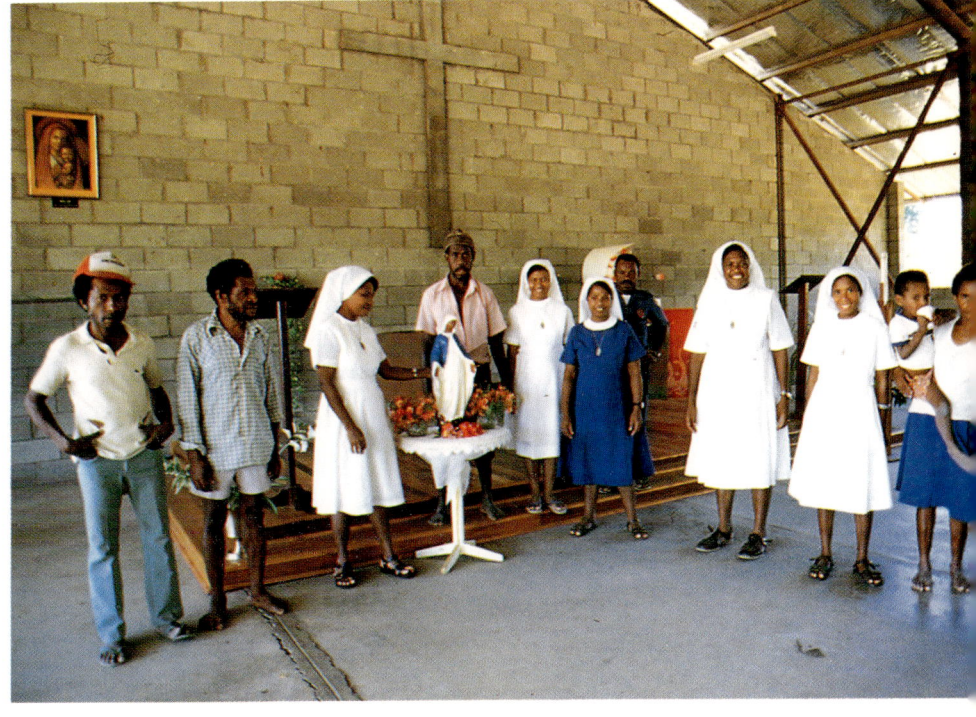

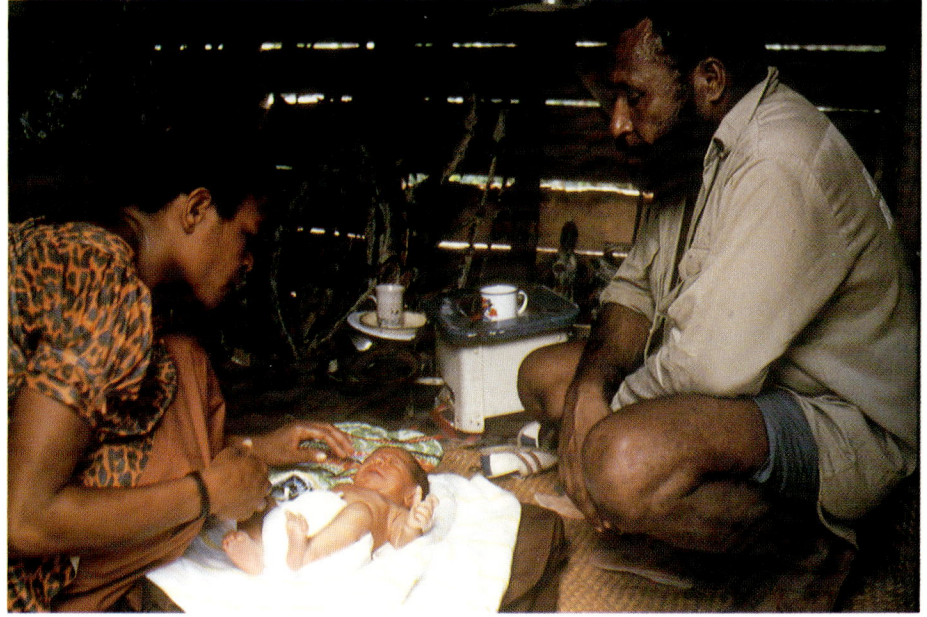

"My *wantoks* may give me five or ten kina to help feed my two wives and ten children and at other times I get some cash welding exhaust pipes back onto cars. However when I do sell my 'works of art' I may get up to two or three thousand kina.

I do most of these metal works out of my pure imagination, i.e., without the aid of a model picture or something else. Others may use models, but I do not; I use my own mind and usually try to introduce some type of traditional or cultural touch with it.

I make things with a story attached to it. I don't just go ahead and come up with anything wild. Everything I do has traditional back-up of one form or another in a story. Never have I made any two works identical in any way. One of my works hangs in the Vice Chancellor's office at the University. And there's a big eagle I made for the American Embassy.

Papua New Guineans do not seem to be interested in my works but many white men buy them. Oh yes, there is another one of my works in the terminal at Jacksons Airport, International Section. I should expect some top shots in PNG to buy something but they haven't — at least not yet.

My very close friends think I am wasting my time. Only when I do get paid do they realise the importance of my works. The money I get from this rubbish seems to be a shock to them."

Ruki Fami, Artist Welder,
Morata, National Capital.

"Most of them are obviously unemployed. You can tell... I mean, you know, they are the ones who spend nearly the whole day here. I see some faces five times a week."

Amusement Centre Attendant, National Capital.

"We sometimes go without lunch when we don't earn enough money. We do feel hungry after having a single piece of fish or bottle of drink, but that's the way it is. It's something we can't help.

We don't always play for leisure. Whenever there is a chance, we play for money. Sometimes we would win as much as ten kina in a single day. We never allow anyone to beat us. We know every game costs money so we always try our best to win every game. But there are exceptions though. When playing with low bets of twenty toea, we let people win three times before offering stakes of a kina or more."

An Unemployed Youth, National Capital.

"I don't think I'll ever get accepted for a decent job because I have no qualifications. By playing snooker, I'm helping myself because no one else in my family has any job in town."

An Unemployed Youth, National Capital.

"After playing for Kone Tigers and then Easts I joined Hobar Wests in 1983 and now I am their captain. It's been a good season for Wests. We won the minor premiership, the grand final and the club championship.

We trained very hard — three hours for three days during each week to be ready for the weekend game.

Sometimes I would go off and do extra training by myself. We have players from different parts of the community in our team — highland and coastal areas — and I think this builds up national unity.

Independence has been a good thing for Papua New Guinea and I think our leaders are doing a good job — it's just that too many parliamentarians are trying to be the 'captain'.

When I first came to Port Moresby I was unemployed for two years but I just kept looking until I got a job with Coca Cola. After serving as a labourer and then an operator they have made me a personnel clerk.

I hate 'rascals' — they do not have the right to steal if they are unemployed. They should go back to their villages. Now the rugby season is over I am coaching some of the unemployed youth at Tokarara to make up a team."

Henry Miro, Rugby Captain, National Capital.

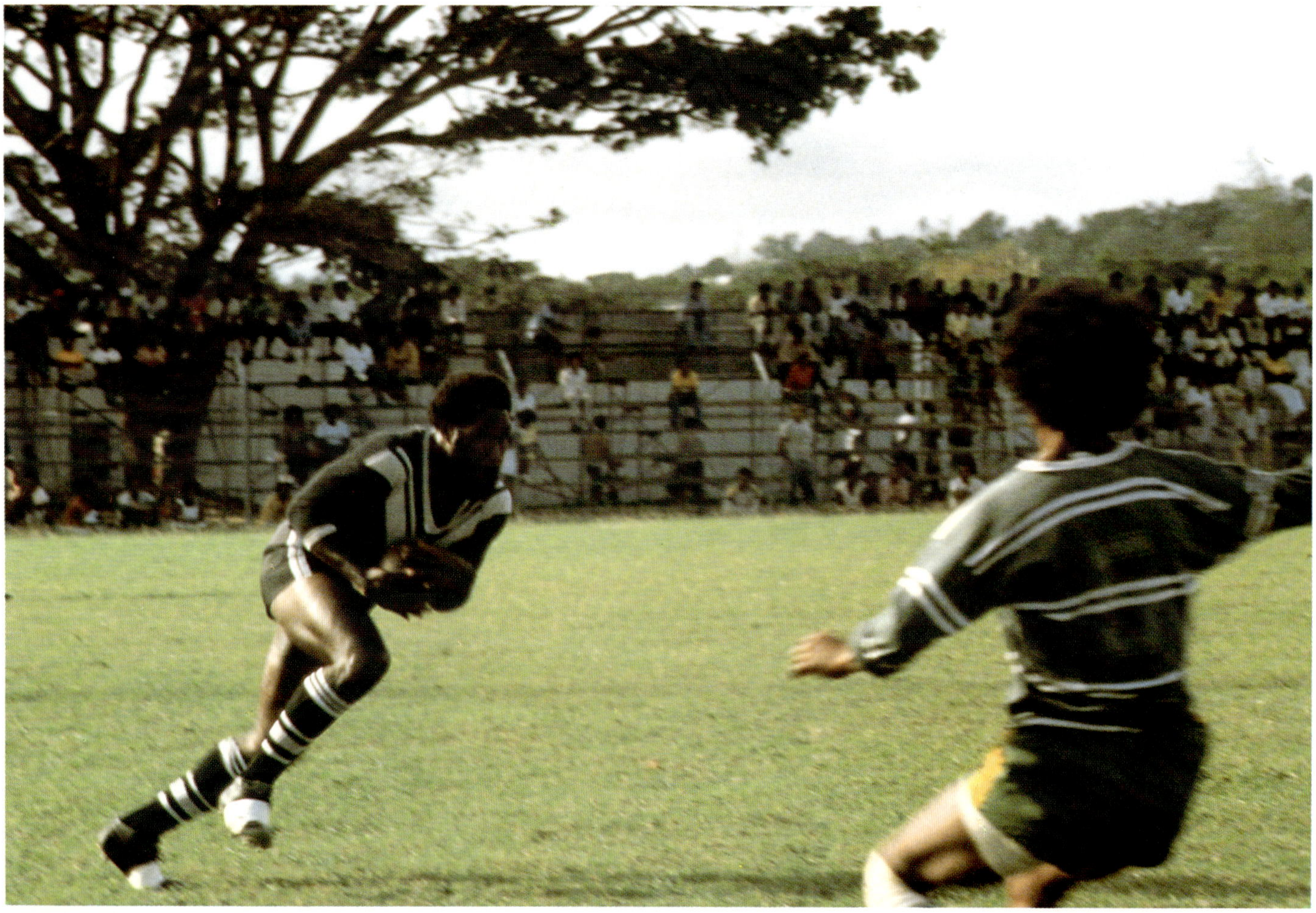

WE SPEAK
THE KINA
LANGUAGE

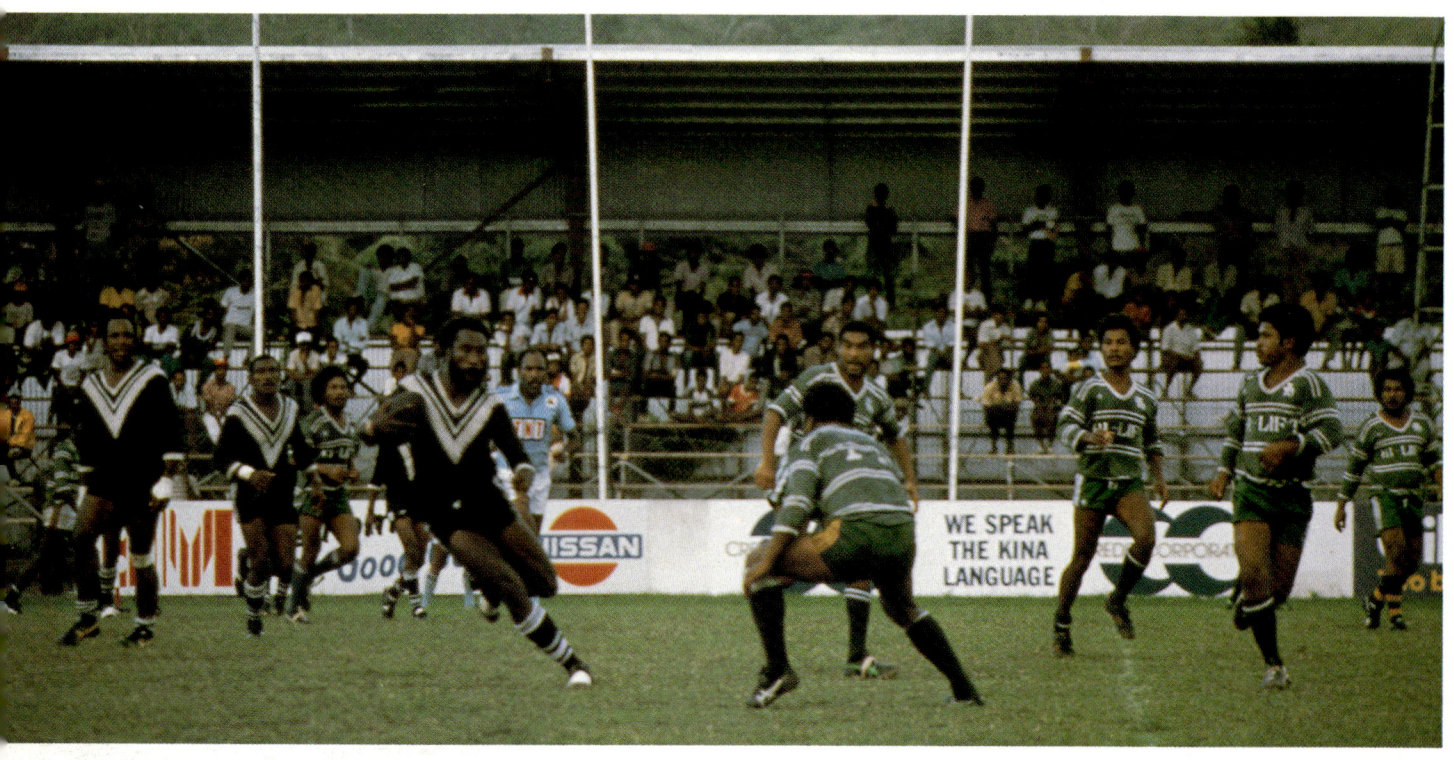

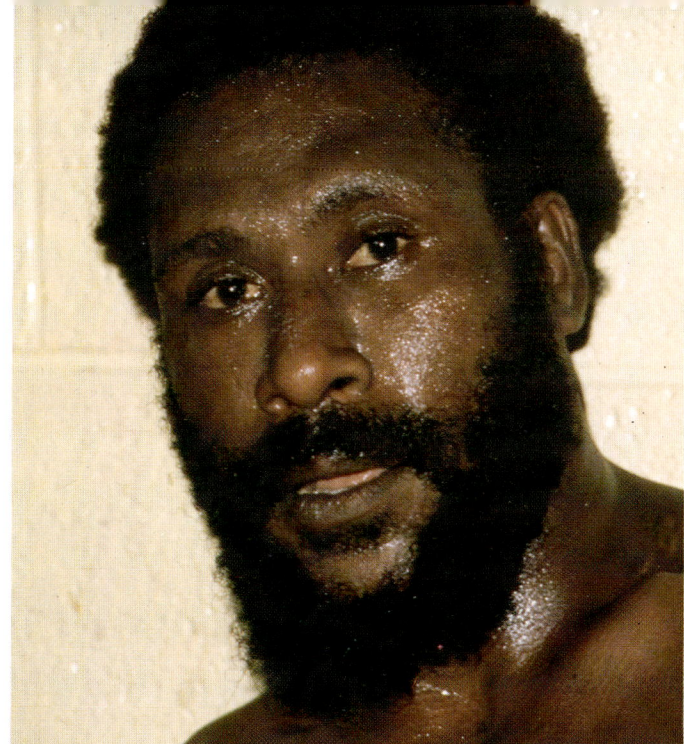

"I used to get scared watching my husband play rugby but now I don't worry because I feel he can look after himself.

I was really happy when Wests won the grand final this year, but the crowd around Henry was so big I couldn't get near him during the celebrations.

My husband and I both have work so we manage to survive in Port Moresby. He works for Coca Cola and I work as a computer operator for Paradise Bakery. We've been trying for four years to obtain a house of our own but we've failed and I doubt if we'll ever succeed."

Mrs Torua Miro.

"I plan to continue in radio journalism for some time because I believe that I play an important role in spreading information to a lot of people. Right now I'm producer of the program 'Contact'. It's a demanding job involving work well beyond normal 'public service' hours and I therefore spend less time with my family.

I interview leading politicians and public servants; the people who actually know how the system should work.

I won't quote anyone in particular but the clear impression I get is that Papua New Guinea has enough money available for the kind of development it needs and there are enough ideas being spelt out — so many experts saying this and that — but we don't have enough of the right kind of manpower. We need people who can get the job done — not just plan or start a project but successfully complete it."

Weni Moka, Radio Journalist, National Capital.

"The concept of the 'extended family' needs to be held onto, even in the cities. If members of our extended family are unemployed then help them; if they need to go back to the village then send them there. Crime starts when this kind of family support breaks down. I hear people say that the only way for the unemployed youth to survive is to steal but that is not the only way. They could go back to the village. The return would require some re-adjustment but they can adjust. It's no use suffering in Port Moresby when there is land, gardens and food in the villages.

I feel like crying when I see children in the cells... you know, these children are lost... the unwanted ones. It's good that there are female members of the police force because we are sensitive to the problems of children and women."

Weni Moka, Reserve Constable, National Capital.

"Close to where I am living now there is a club to which I go. I have met so many people from Australia and other areas too, like Greeks — very good people. Everybody seems friendly and helpful. When some people are drunk they ask me silly questions, but it is all in good humour.

My wife found it hard during the first couple of weeks, because she cannot speak English. She was frightened but I told her she shouldn't be. She is finding it easier now. Soon she will be taking English lessons. When we shop we have been able to find the same kinds of food that we are used to. We were very happy to find out that *kaukau* is available down here.

I am quite proud of our Independence. I like Michael Somare. Some people don't, but that's a personal choice. I am proud there was no trouble during the time we gained Independence. The country has its problems but if we work together we will be able to sort them out. We have worked hard during our first ten years, and have now built a base on which to build a good nation. The next ten years will be very exciting for Papua New Guinea. We must all work together.

My family and I enjoy living in Melbourne, the weather at the moment is cold but not as cold as we had been told. I find that here money is more important than in Mendi. At home, if I didn't have money, a bunch of bananas would appear from my village or a load of *kaukau*."

Paulus Kombo, Announcer,
Radio Australia, Melbourne.

181

"Our studio has a 24-track recorder and a 32-channel mixer — the only equipment of its kind in Papua New Guinea. It enables us to route the music of individual instruments on to the master tape and to adjust the volume and tone for each. We can add and subtract and polish until we get a perfect mix, to produce a cassette for commercial release.

I am also a member of a band called the 'Junior Unbelievers' and we have been performing throughout East New Britain during the last couple of years. We sing in English, *Tok Pisin* and traditional languages. *Tok Pisin* is a great language. The public understands and responds so easily to what it says."

Gordon Gaius, Recording Engineer, East New Britain.

"I played with 'April Sun' and 'Vibrations' before joining 'Barike'.
The stuff we record is based mainly on market tastes. Although I prefer heavy stuff, we record more country and western and it sure sells fast."

John Wong, Musician,
East New Britain.

"I hear stories and I put them to music. Some of my songs are about young people, and love, and marriage and divorce too. I have also composed songs about the volcano — the *maunten paia,* fights and car accidents. When I sung with a group called *'Painim Wok'* and I wrote songs about young people looking for work and not finding it.

Traditional Tolai melodies are combined with foreign tunes: Rock 'n roll, heavy metal, country and western styles are mixed up in our songs.

I was a government clerk for five years before becoming a professional musician. That was eight years ago and I have been interested to note the way in which bands have developed their own distinctive styles during these years."

George Telek, Composer and Musician,
East New Britain.

"I was still a child when we obtained Independence and I have grown up with the changes, so I'm not in a good position to compare 'before' with 'after'.

I am now working on a film which features a housewife, tied down to daily routines, fetching water, washing, cleaning, cooking... going to bed well after everyone else. My film is trying to show that women must

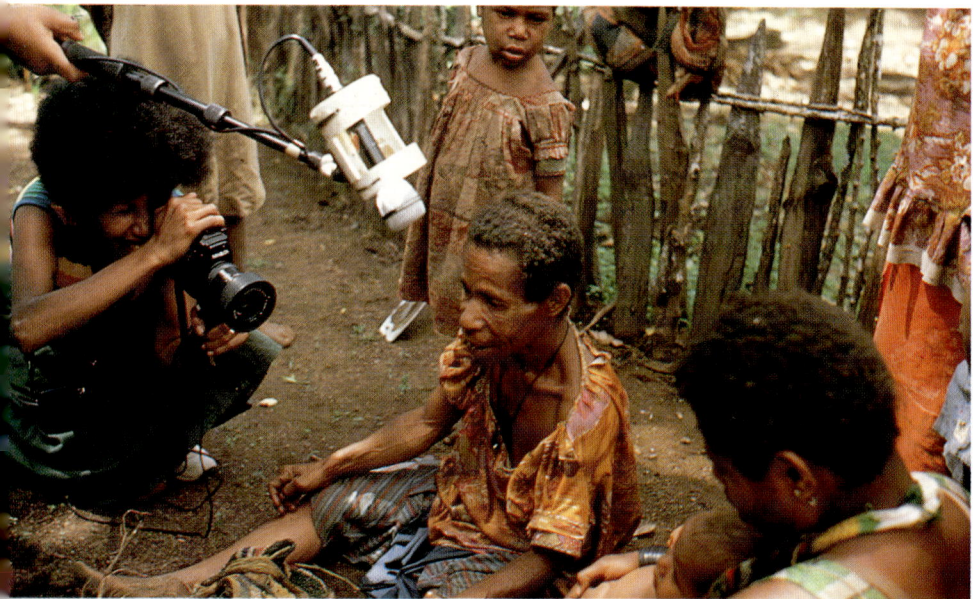

solve their own problems and stand more united. I often think about women such as prostitutes, who are considered dirty by society and how they can be helped.

Talking about women's problems, I am no exception. My enrolment at the *'Skul Bilong Wokim Piksa'* was at the expense of my own marriage. I felt that I could do more with my life through the 'know how' I receive here, than by being a mere housewife."

"When I came to the *'Skul Bilong Wokim Piksa'* I was disappointed. I had expected a luxurious, Hollywood type of studio where everything would be available at the touch of a button. But no, the one and only building was used as office and classroom. The editing room during the day was my bedroom at night. I felt like leaving but decided to stay and give it a go and I'm glad I did.

We're only making documentary films at the moment but I'd like to move into feature films because local audiences seem to respond to them better. They could be used to both entertain and educate.

I have enjoyed travelling with the Raun Raun Theatre Company. During their 'Popular Theatre Campaign', they presented a series of educational plays on such topics as family planning and nutrition. After the plays discussions were encouraged among the audience. We would tape the play and the discussion and screen them back to reinforce the message."

Leonie Kanawi, Trainee Film Maker, Eastern Highlands.

"I am a trained school teacher and I played the role of a village teacher in 'Tukana'. I had no experience in acting so I felt nervous. Albert Toro and Chris Owen encouraged me and all the members of the cast worked well together."

Regina Tulsa, Film Actress, North Solomons.

"I was very excited when I saw my daughter acting in the 'Tukana' film. At the end of the film she died — but I knew she wasn't really dead and I want her to make a new film."

Catherine, Regina Tulsa's mother, North Solomons.

"With the National Theatre Company we travelled the world; an experience that broadened my outlook.

I also developed my writing talent which I used as a means of getting extra cash for the house. I wasn't earning a salary that was adequate enough to cater for such a young family as mine. I was asked to write the dialogue for the film 'Tukana'.

The final draft was accepted and we went into making the film in 1980. Most of the film was a part of the life that I had gone through: you know, leaving school, going to the mine, being a drunk, smoker and

womaniser — but not too much of that.

Most people, even my wife, say that I was really acting myself out, which in a way is true, but sometimes it still irritates me to hear them call me Tukana. In fact, acting in the film has helped me become a different sort of person; not that fake plastic man on the screen.

Now I'm trying to run a theatre company with support from the government; both provincial and national. We have presented some drama including two musicals, 'Ipi Tombi' and 'Jesus Christ Superstar' I still write for the *Arawa Bulletin* and I enjoy highlighting contemporary issues particularly the problems of this transitional era in our Nation's development. My style is a 'gad-fly' sort of thing; attacking here and there and flying away."

Albert Toro, Actor, Writer, Musician, North Solomons.

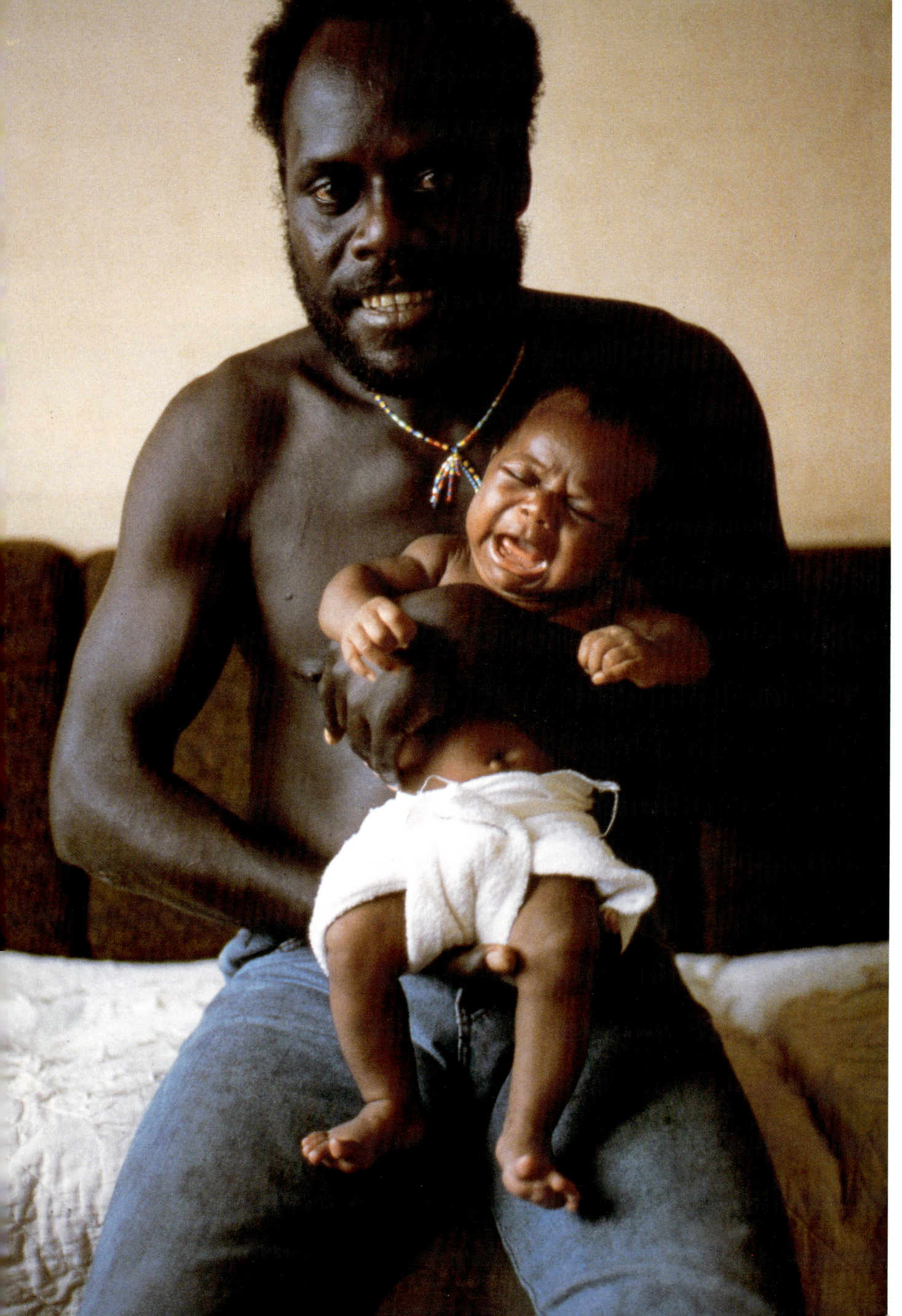

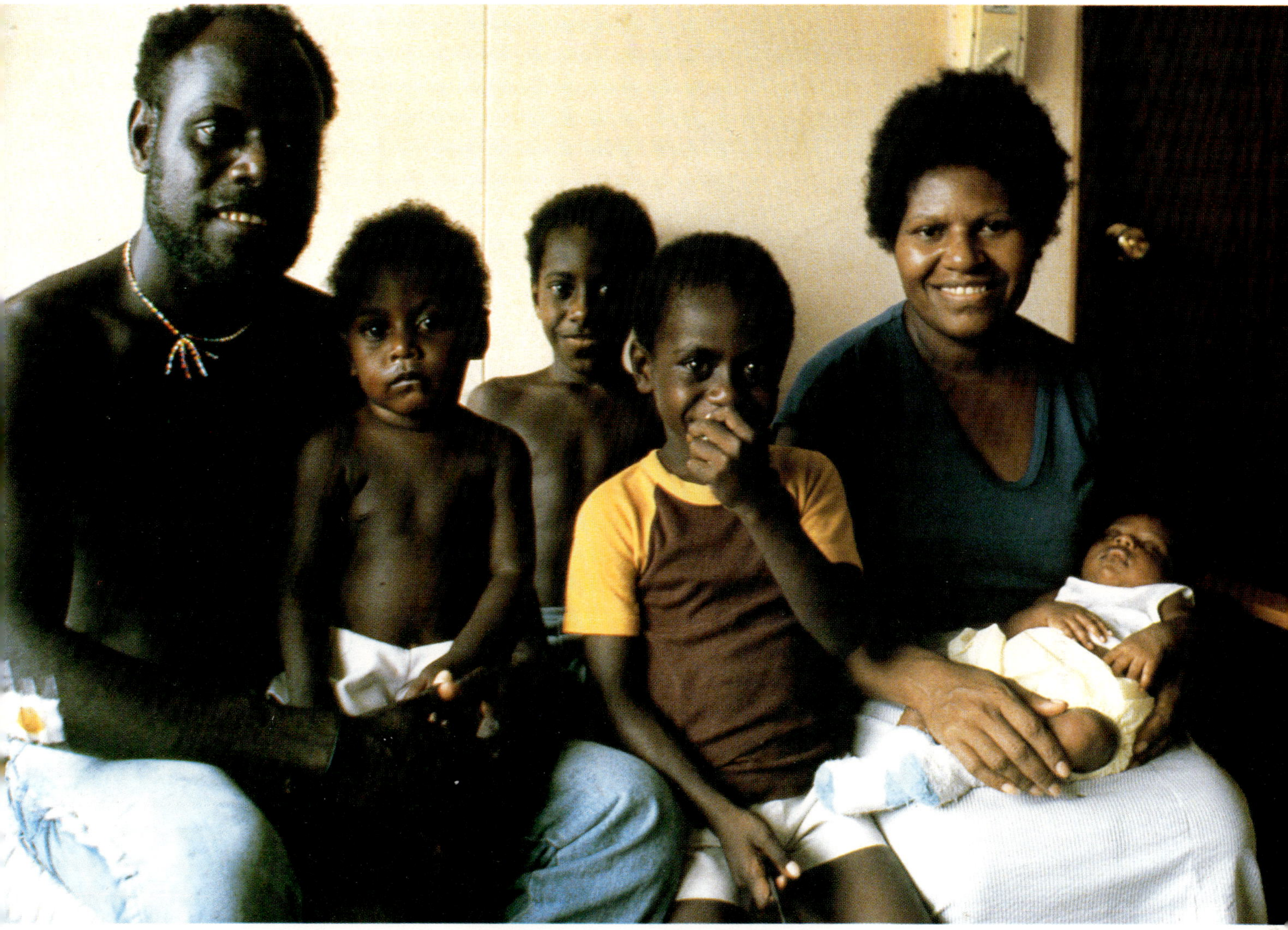

"The granting of Independence can be compared with taking the yokes off the backs of some bullocks. Not used to such freedom they run round wildly, stampede and some get hurt in the process. We now have freedom but at some cost to ourselves. We don't know how to discipline ourselves. We are misusing our rights and privileges."

I think the main focus should be on family life. If you have a stable family the members do not go running around causing trouble and damaging themselves. Unstable families cause an unstable society and an unstable society leads to unstable government."

Anita Toro, Film Actress, North Solomons.

"I would certainly like to act in another film if the role is meaningful. I'd like to act the role of a housewife or someone who is being victimised. Women don't speak out much and films are a media that can successfully get their message across. What is life like in a home situation? People don't see what goes on behind closed doors. They just see the sort of masked faces people wear out in the street.

"If I was the Prime Minister I would introduce a lot of changes. First I would get rid of the party system and require all political parties to work together as a team. I would encourage Local Government but abolish Provincial Government. The size of the Public Service would be reduced by getting rid of inefficient bureaucrats. I believe in small-scale industries and village based projects and would promote these rather than large-scale town based industries. To achieve this I would liberalise the lending policies of the banks. While I realise that education is very important, I am very sad when I see unemployed youth. The only solution is to develop a scheme whereby all school leavers are allocated a piece of land and some capital to develop it."

Ru Kundil, Western Highlands.

"Before the white man came, a man who had many pigs and wives, a man who led tribal fights, made good public speeches at ceremonies, a man who worked hard and fed other people, he was recognised as a true leader and was respected for his achievements. His ability to do these things was talked about by his people as well as by other tribes.

Leaders of today should realise that being educated or holding a responsible position in government does not entitle them to recognition and respect. These they must earn for themselves by their achievements."

Sir Wamp Wan, Western Highlands.

"All of our leaders – local, provincial and national must be educated. I don't mean that they should receive formal education but they must learn of the consequences of fighting, they must learn of the consequences of mis-management, they must learn of the consequences of political corruption. Members of Parliament should go to the people, sit down with them and be educated by them. The politicians tend to rely too much on giving handouts but this encourages people to become parasites – to do nothing for themselves and to expect more."

Peter Paraki, Enga.

"When we attained Independence a lot of people seemed to slacken their efforts. They seemed to think that having attained Independence they could just take it easy. Okay, we are independent but we've got to be self-reliant; we've got to produce more of our own food like rice and sugar. People don't usually look at it from that point of view. What this country needs is people with drive. History tells us that in Australia and America development hangs on a few people; it's the few people that try and lead the nation. They invest their effort and money. They give employment, they build bridges and roads. But right now in this country people are saying – 'Hurray, we're independent!' and they look to the government for free handouts. That's wrong. Whenever there is a landslide, drought or a flood we just cry to the government. There are some genuine requests but there's a tendency to develop a 'cargo cult' sort of attitude. For the next ten years I would like to see Papua New Guinea expand the agricultural sector and perhaps get into manufacturing a bit more. I am not talking about heavy industries as we will not be able to compete with Australia and Japan. I want to see Papua New Guinea develop its agricultural resources and its human skills. I think we could provide Asia with all the food they need if we had the right agricultural program."

Peter Kama Kerpi, Simbu.

"Papua New Guineans have a great potential to develop the country and themselves but they are just too lazy. If we had more money we might be able to develop our country much more. Timber and fish and a lot of other very good things are asking to be developed. When we entered into Independence I was anticipating serious trouble but this did not eventuate at all. I am very proud about that. I really do hope that in the next ten years Papua New Guinea will become a better place. The government, too, must start taking strict measures with the lazy public servants. They have to be there at 8am and finish at 4pm. At present its 8.30am to 3.30pm, 'government time'. Time is money and public servants are robbing public money. We say we have money problems and yet we steal it from ourselves. Time is a very important asset being grossly misused in Papua New Guinea. Papua New Guineans must learn to stop stealing from themselves."

Auwo Ketauwo,
Eastern Highlands.

"In the past ten years a lot of things have changed. Before Independence things were a bit better; the education system was good; the public service was effective and politicians were more honest and reliable. After Independence it seems that the education standard has dropped, the public service has become ineffective and there aren't any more reliable politicians. If this continues I don't know what the country is going to be like in five to ten years' time. When I consider these things, I am not particularly concerned about myself as a successful, self-employed individual, but I think there would have been a lot more like me if we were not burdened with a 'sick' and 'ineffective' public service full of people with a poor education who don't want to see bright people with talents progressing beyond them. Promotion should be on ability and merit and not through the *wantok* system or political appointments."

Edward Piawe,
Southern Highlands.

"I am happy with Papua New Guinea being Independent. We have to learn from our mistakes and Papua New Guinea, like other Pacific islands, needs to be given chances. We have to learn our weaknesses. The Government isn't doing everything perfectly but it is a hard job. We are now starting from the 'grass roots' trying to become like other countries and Independence is not an easy thing. Of course the mistakes the politicians make are there for everyone to see and everyone is ready to criticise the government when that happens. I think we have to steer the government in the right direction. If we don't, then we shouldn't blame them."

Lahui Tau, National Capital.

"Over the last ten years I have noticed that the development of this country has been slow. I think this is because there are too many plans and too much abstract theorising without realistic concrete planning. There should be more effort in the development of cocoa, coffee and copra if the economy is to be stable. I do not think we should rely too much on minerals because they can all be dug out of the ground tomorrow and then what will we do? Young people growing up should be diverted to acquire skills and to appreciate how they can become part of the economy. They should be taught to live in a rural environment and adjust their living standards to the rural area. The present school system develops too many false expectations. It should be reformed to concentrate on preparing children for a useful life and to accept proper moral values. When I was at school, we would be in classes in the morning and work physically in the afternoon. We had to work for our own food. We worked in the gardens and grew rice and vegetables. We didn't beg food from anybody; food was produced by ourselves, for ourselves; and that was good education. In the next ten years the people must be willing to work physically and really put their efforts into developing themselves and the nation. The people of today are becoming lazy. We are educating them to expect and see an illusion. Illusions are fabricated concepts that do not really exist.

The government should make Papua New Guinea a multi-racial society so that people of all ages, and races can live and work together in this country."

Henry Moses, North Solomons.

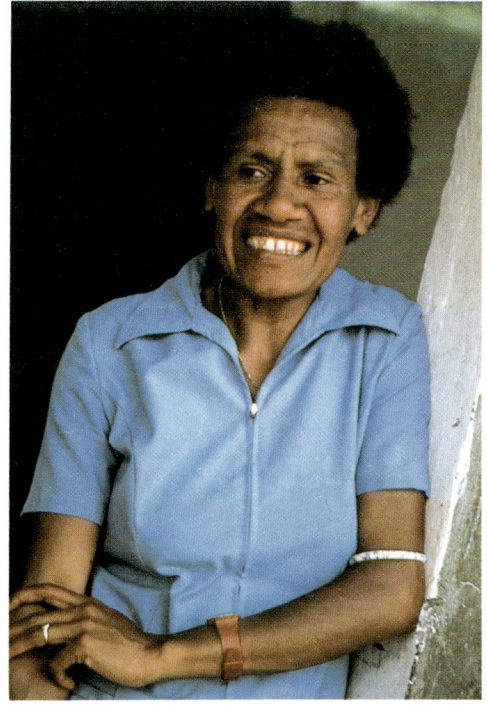

"I don't think enough emphasis is being done to help people work for basic development and fundamental things in the community. Everybody is talking about new roads and new bridges and what kind of new cash based business they want to start up. I say there should be more emphasis on just developing a person to become the kind of citizen this country needs.

Angela Soso, Eastern Highlands.

"North Solomons Province was the first to get its own Provincial Government so that people could rule themselves. Many others have also got theirs since then. A few provinces have been seen as not being able to govern themselves but this doesn't mean they don't have the ability. They just need to learn. North Solomons tried and succeeded and I give credit to Father Momis and others who fought for decentralisation in the first place. After ten years of Independence I am happy that the people of the provinces, have been given the chance to govern themselves — to set up little governments of our own that are similar to the Australian State Governments. Many provinces have proven that Port Moresby is just the headquarters and that they are prepared and capable of looking after themselves, nearer home. But the most important thing is that we should have a bit more commitment in the next ten years. There has been too much irresponsibility displayed. Problems of rascalism and so on are increasing because the people are not seeing themselves as Papua New Guineans. They're seeing themselves as individuals. And when someone doesn't have something that someone else has, he knocks someone's teeth out to get it."

Patrick Itta, North Solomons.

"After Independence ten years ago I spent seven years out of the country. On my return I was amazed to see that we have been able to maintain the democracy in the system. It was my view that the political situation at the time was so unstable but it has proved that it was able to survive. One of the things that worries me, however, is that we are not progressing economically. It annoys me to see so much corruption going on – the whole public service system and the political system is very ineffective in my view. If Papua New Guinea wants to go anywhere in the future, they need to decentralise the public service and give greater control to the people at the provincial level and try to maintain some kind of efficiency at that level. It's extremely difficult to control a huge body at the national level especially when you don't have the calibre of people required to make effective decisions."

Joseph Herman, Morobe.

"I for one see Independence as something very good for Papua New Guinea. We have taken responsibility on our shoulders and are not expecting others to do the work for us. Independence has been good for us. I don't really know about the future, for I am not the type of person to really think about it a lot. However I do hope that Papua New Guinea will become a better place to live in. At the moment I am saddened by the rate of crime seen in the country. Nevertheless like any other country we have to face both the good and the bad. I am concerned about children in general as well as my own children. I want a good future for them.

I would like to see a change in the attitudes of our leaders particularly the politicians. They are always picking on one another's faults and disregarding important problems. I usually turn the radio off because the news of their behaviour is too childish. I think it is the leaders who should set a better example for the people. The lawmakers are the ones who seem to break the law and the innocent people suffer. That is how I see it."

Gladys Yadiwillo,
Eastern Highlands.

"This is my country and I will not give up encouraging it to go ahead. We are a young country and we have only just started. We are making mistakes but we are moving forward. The people must talk more among themselves and share their ideas so we can understand and encourage one another. The people are the roots of the tree. Unless we use our own power and our own skills and enable each Papua New Guinean to make his own contribution we will be independent in name only. Together we can move away from our colonial past and grow into a good, well developed country and establish friendly relationships with our neighbours."

John Teosin, North Solomons.

"The Germans were here until the Australians forced them out. Then the Japanese came and forced the Australians out. Then Australia came back with America.

The Germans were before my time, but I've worked for the Japanese and the Australians and now we're independent. To be independent you've got to be strong and work hard. If you just sit down and expect things to happen you'll find you have no money.

I've been a cook at Brandi High School for years and years. I remember when Michael Somare and Tony Bais were school boys. Now when they see me they say 'So you're still here — you're not dead yet?' and I say 'So you're getting too fat — you're drinking too much beer!"

Gabriel Koapi, Cook,
Brandi High School, East Sepik.

"You may be a very powerful man but when you are in the village people expect you to share what you have. You can contribute work, or food, or shell money, or cash, but you must contribute. In the major cities some individuals who have moved well away from the traditional village barter system and into the monetary system have become rich. In the village it is different. You may have a plantation of coffee, cocoa or coconut trees but these are more important as status symbols. Because, no matter how much is earned from them and no matter what is bought with the earnings, in the long run, it is all shared."

"My village is on a sand bank among the mangroves around the lake and the water is brackish. A well is necessary if fresh water is to be drawn from deeper down. I asked the Public Works Department to install one but they never came

around. So we decided to do it ourselves. I bought some cement and gravel and two concrete cylinders — they all had to be carried in from Wewak. From Lae I bought a couple of hand pumps so now we'll have a better water supply for the whole village.

I have been the head of the Government since the beginning and there is not one single thing belonging to the Government in my village. If other people are frustrated, I have the same kind of frustration. But if I put something in my village first — what would people say about me?"

Michael Somare,
Karau Village, East Sepik.

"My own father, who left to become a policeman when he was young, did not have much to do with the traditions of the village. It was my Uncle Saub who passed the traditions and values on to me. He was responsible for my initiation, for teaching me about our clan, our totems, our music and about the responsibilities of chieftancy."

"Years ago, when I worked for the Australian Administration, I used to do all my own cooking and I still like to cook, so I help Veronica from time to time. I help her in the garden too but I don't work as hard as she does."

"Our country must, of course, change. But many of the values our varied communities shared in the past will remain with us as guiding principles in the future.

Despite the pressures on us from the outside world, Papua New Guineans will succeed, in the end, in building a society in which decision making is a communal process — a society believing in the sharing of wealth rather than possessed by the mad spirit of competition characteristic of the Western world."

Michael Somare, *Sana*, 1975.

AFTERWORDS

It has been a difficult but fascinating assignment to select and present a range of faces and voices that are broadly representative of the people of Papua New Guinea during the tenth year of their nationhood. The majority of those finally included in this book were selected because they illustrate ways of life and attitudes that can be recognised as typically Papua New Guinean. But the book does not restrict portrayal to what is typical. The nation encompasses high degrees of diversity and dynamic processes of change that must also be represented. Thus, attempts to define the people according to common types or shared attributes would be inappropriate — as well as futile.

This is an anniversary publication so it contains studies of a number of individuals whose outstanding achievements since Independence are worthy of note. Much has been said or attempted in the name of "development" or "progress" during the last decade and it therefore seemed important that some of the successful forerunners be included — along with some of those who have not yet entered the race, and some who have dropped out.

Some individuals were selected on the recommendation of fellow citizens. Some were selected after chance encounters with the photographers or the editor. For every one person finally included in the book, many who are equally interesting could not be. It is to be regretted that the limited space available did not allow a wider sample. At the outset, a decision was made to exclude politicians and senior public servants in favour of less frequently publicised people. The exception is Michael Somare but he is portrayed here, not in his role as the Prime Minister, but as a villager.

Those included have not been classified or divided into chapters. The sequence of the book mixes the ordinary and the extraordinary, the young and the old, the villager and the city dweller, the farmer, the businessman, the employed and the unemployed. But the arrangement of subjects is not random and the reader may find additional interest in discerning the progression of visual and textual themes. There are also interesting contrasts and ironies for those who can discover them.

While most of the views expressed in this book reflect pride in individual and national achievements, there are many expressions of concern and criticism. Some people believe that all is not well with the Nation and have no hesitation in speaking their minds. In so doing they remind us that Papua New Guinea, with its democratic government and free press is a remarkably open society.

Many glossy books have been produced to illustrate the wonderful scenery and colourful aspects of the cultures of Papua New Guinea — and why not? But too often the perspectives and interests have been conditioned by the appeal of the exotic to foreign audiences. This book is an attempt to more closely represent contemporary reality in a manner that may be appreciated both within and without the Nation.

Family photos are very popular in Papua New Guinea homes. You should approach this book as its sub-title suggests — a national family album.

ELTON BRASH

CREDITS

EDITOR:	Elton Brash.
EDITORIAL ADVISORS:	Sir Seselo Abel, Dennis O'Rourke, Jose Reis.
PHOTOGRAPHERS:	Jose Reis, Eisuke Shimauchi.
INTERVIEWERS:	Jose Reis, Patrick Matbob, Elton Brash; Samson Chicki, John Kasaipwalova, Joseph Ketan, Daniel Kumbon, Steven Mago, Tapei Martin, Chris Owen, Dave Peterson, Vere Ravu, Rocky Roe, Ebon Samky, Samson Tatakali, Maggie Wilson.
LAYOUT:	Jose Reis with assistance from Vagoli Bouauka, Gabi Boutau, Vagi Raula and Ted Vagi.
TRANSLATORS:	Samson Tatakali, Samson Waka Chicki, Habia Babe, Joseph Ketan, Daniel Kumbon, Alex Mitaharo, Ebo Samky, Basil Tabel, Johnson Tia and Justin Yatu.
FIELD ASSISTANTS:	Habia Babe, Roger Dickson, Joseph Ketan, Daniel Kumbon, Tapel Martin, Alex Mitaharo, Vere Ravu, Ebo Samky, Samson Tatakali, Valentine Win, Maggie Wilson.
ADDITIONAL PHOTOGRAPHS:	David Peterson, Rocky Roe.
AIR TRAVEL:	TALAIR, with special thanks to Stewart Forsythe, Brinley Waddell and Violet Gibson.
WORD PROCESSOR SUPPLIED BY:	Daltron Electronics.
KEYBOARD STAFF:	Rachel Noah, Angela Paura, Didrie Nano.
PROJECT SECRETARY:	Bronwyn Stewart.
10TH ANNIVERSARY EXHIBITION:	Joseph Naguwean, Vincent Gulasini, Catherine de Courcy.

ACKNOWLEDGEMENTS

The production of this book was funded by the Government of Papua New Guinea, on the recommendation of the Tenth Anniversary of Independence Advisory Committee. The interest and support of Mr Andrew Yauieb, Mr Michael Komtagorea, Mr Tom Ritako, Mr Leith Anderson and Superintendent David Pringuer are gratefully acknowledged.

Mr Jose Reis and Mr Eisuke Shimauchi accepted the commission at short notice and worked tirelessly to complete it. Mr Jose Reis has contributed creatively to all aspects of the production.

The production project was based at the University of Papua New Guinea and many of its staff assisted. Joe Naguwean, Vincent Gulaseni and Catherine de Courcy set up the exhibition at the University Library during the Anniversary Celebrations to display samples of the material now contained in this book. Members of the Geography Department, including Geoff Humphrey, Gabi Boutau, Vagoli Bouauka and Vagi Raula, were particularly helpful.

TALAIR provided generous discount air fares and a reliable ticketing service.

THE TIMES OF PAPUA NEW GUINEA kindly released Mr Patrick Matbob from duties to enable him to accompany Mr Shimauchi in the field. Mr Matbob's perceptive interviews provided an important part of the material for the text.

DALTRON ELECTRONICS offered a generous discount on word processing equipment.

Provincial Governments provided advice and logistic support to the photographers and interviewers through their respective secretariats.

But the real credit belongs to the many people of Papua New Guinea who agreed to be interviewed and photographed. They make up this book and it is dedicated to them.

Elton Brash

BIOGRAPHICAL NOTES

Elton Brash:

Worked as a teacher, lecturer and educational administrator for twenty five years in Papua New Guinea. His academic interests are in literature of new nations. He proposed and co-ordinated the production of this book as a contribution to the celebration of the Tenth Anniversary of Papua New Guinea's attainment of Independence.

Patrick Matbob:

From the Madang Province. Trained in music at the National Arts School but is now a journalist and writer with "The Times of Papua New Guinea."

Jose Reis:

Graduated in Photography from the City of Birmingham Poly-technic and in Social Science from the University of Birmingham. Since 1976 he has been a freelance photo-journalist working in Portugal, France and England. He was awarded the Photokina Obelisc 1968 by the German Commission for UNESCO and in 1979, The Bradford Centenary Photographic Commission funded by the Arts Council of Great Britain.

He has held one man exhibitions in England and Portugal and contributed to collective ones in Spain, West Germany, U.S.S.R., England, Italy and Portugal.

His work is included in the public collections of the Bibliothèque Nationale de Paris, Bradford Art Galleries and Museums and the New Guinea Collection of the Library of the University of Papua New Guinea. Mr Reis is also editor of "Fotografia Portuguesa, 1970-1980", Lisbon, 1982.

Eisuke Shimauchi:

After graduating from Nihon University in Tokyo he entered Kobonsha Publishing as a resident photographer. Later he transferred to Hebonsha Publishing as a photographer for Taiyo (The Sun) Magazine.

Now he is a freelance photographer concentrating on feature reporting.

Mr Shimauchi is a member of the Japan Professional Photographers' Association and the Japan Travel Writers' Organisation. He has travelled widely in Europe and Asia and has held two major exhibitions featuring photographs of France and two exhibitions on Japanese themes. Two collections of his pictures have been published – "Bonjour Paris!" and "Yoshino River Revisited After Twenty Years Absence."

INDEX

Page No.	Name of Subject	Province	Photographer	Interviewer
2TC	Albert and Michelle Toro	North Solomons	Jose Reis	
2TL	Mary Jua	Manus	Eisuke Shimauchi	
2TR	Jacob Nirab	Morobe	Eisuke Shimauchi	
2ML	Thomas Billy	Madang	Eisuke Shimauchi	
2MR	Tawanda Market	Southern Highlands	Jose Reis	
2BL	James Muli	Southern Highlands	Jose Reis	
2BR	Wabali Aiya	Southern Highlands	Jose Reis	
3TL	Sing Sing	Western Highlands	Jose Reis	
3TR	Michael Somare	East Sepik	Jose Reis	
3BL	Piru	Southern Highands	Jose Reis	
3BC	Tege Bobole	Southern Highlands	Jose Reis	
3BR	Depen Kanai	Morobe	Eisuke Shimauchi	
4-5	Market	Enga	Eisuke Shimauchi	
6-7	Depen Kanai	Morobe	Eisuke Shimauchi	Patrick Matbob
8	Siasu Martin	New Ireland	Jose Reis	Jose Reis
9	Soso Siwi	Eastern Highlands	Jose Reis	Jose Reis
10-11	Kepas Kepkali Kemb	Enga	Eisuke Shimauchi	Daniel Kumbon
12-16	Tribal Flight	Southern Highlands	Jose Reis	Jose Reis Samson Tatakali
17	Sir Wamp Wan	Western Highlands	Jose Reis	Jose Reis Maggie Wilson
18-19	Garoinedi Tariowai	Milne Bay	Eisuke Shimauchi	Patrick Matbob
20-21	Bariagua Mondoli	Southern Highlands	Jose Reis	Jose Reis Habia Babe
22-27	Kaprau family	New Ireland	Jose Reis	Jose Reis
28-31	Ru Kandil	Western Highlands	Jose Reis	Jose Reis Joseph Ketan
32	Chief Nalubutau Beona	Milne Bay	Elsuke Shimauchi	John Kasaipwalova
33	MacDonald Atu	Oro	Elsuke Shimauchi	Patrick Matbob
34-35	Koni Nurara Tondu Wallmini	East Sepik	Jose Reis	Jose Reis
36	Willie Ber	Madang	Eisuke Shimauchi	Patrick Matbob Jose Reis/ Vere Ravu
37-41	Au Gewa	Central	Jose Reis	
42-43	John Tonte	West Sepik	Jose Reis	Jose Reis
44-45	Marame Peke	Simbu	Jose Reis	Jose Reis
46-47	Matane Eliakim	West New Britain	Eisuke Shimauchi	Patrick Matbob
48-49	Asiba Imesung Gumoi Puki	Western	Eisuke Shimauchi	Patrick Matbob
50-53	McKenzie Kamoa	Oro	Eisuke Shimauchi	Elton Brash
54-55	Peter Peraki	Enga	Eisuke Shimauchi	Samson Chicki
56-57	Kaypsolin Raipo	Morobe	Eisuke Shimauchi	Patrick Matbob
58-59	Jacob Nirab	Morobe	Eisuke Shimauchi	Patrick Matbob
60-61	Omas Genora	Morobe	Eisuke Shimauchi	Patrick Matbob
62-64	Holika Inoke	Milne Bay	Eisuke Shimauchi	Patrick Matbob
65-67	Thomas Billy	Madang	Eisuke Shimauchi	Patrick Matbob
68-69	John Bolemark	Manus	Eisuke Shimauchi	Patrick Matbob
70-71	Ikun Austrai	Manus	Eisuke Shimauchi	Patrick Matbob
72-73	Mary Jua	Manus	Eisuke Shimauchi	Patrick Matbob
74-75	Daniel Dalau	Madang	Eisuke Shimauchi	Patrick Matbob
76-77	Daniel Dalau	Southern Highlands	Jose Reis	Jose Reis
78-79	Peter Tugo	Simbu	Jose Reis	Jose Reis
80-81	Toaripi Toaripi	Gulf	Jose Reis	Jose Reis
82-83	Peter Kama Kerpi	Simbu	Jose Reis	Jose Reis
84-93	Moka Series	Western Highlands	Jose Reis	Jose Reis/ Joseph Ketan
93TR	Ongka Kaipa			
94-95	Apere Goso	Eastern Highlands	Jose Reis	Jose Reis
96-97	Auwo Ketauwo	Eastern Highlands	Jose Reis	Jose Reis
98-99	Betty Ketauwo	Eastern Highlands	Jose Reis	Jose Reis
100-101	Lahui Tau	National Capital	Eisuke Shimauchi	Patrick Matbob
102	Balume Barlagua	Southern Highlands	Jose Reis	Jose Reis/ Habia Babe
103	Wabali Alya	Southern Highlands	Jose Reis	Jose Reis/ Habia Babe
104	Yanabe Tawa	Southern Highlands	Jose Reis	Jose Reis/ Habia Babe
105	Tege Baloboe	Southern Highlands	Jose Reis	Jose Reis/ Habia Babe
106B	Ngini Ariola	Southern Highlands	Jose Reis	Jose Reis Habia Babe
106T-107	Diniim Ngabe	Southern Highlands	Jose Reis	Jose Reis/ Habia Babe
108-109	John Kali	West New Britain	Eisuke Shimauchi	Patrick Matbob
110-111	Joseph Herman	Madang	Rocky Roe	Rocky Roe
112-113	Memoi Matei	West New Britain	Eisuke Shimauchi	Patrick Matbob
114-115	Meremi Maina	Western	Eisuke Shimauchi	Patrick Matbob
116	Luke Yabaria	Southern Highlands	Jose Reis	Jose Reis/ Samson Tatakali

Page No.	Name of Subject	Province	Photographer	Interviewer
120-123	Borok Pitalok	Western	Jose Reis	Chris Owen
124-125	Patrick Itta	North Solomons	Jose Reis	Jose Reis
126-127	Henry Moses	North Solomons	Jose Reis	Jose Reis
128-131	Gesengu Tangii	Southern Highlands	Jose Reis	Jose Reis/ Samson Tatakali
132-135	Peter Kankonaru	Morobe	Eisuke Shimauchi	Patrick Matbob
136-139	Benjamin Talai	East New Britain	Jose Reis	Jose Reis
140-141	Jerry Singirok	West Sepik	Jose Reis	Jose Reis
142-143	Jim Yer	Simbu	Jose Reis	Jose Reis
144-145	Toka Daina Yer	Simbu	Jose Reis	Jose Reis
146	Ruth Saovana-Spriggs	North Solomons	Jose Reis	Jose Reis
147	Rachel Kaetavara	North Solomons	Jose Reis	Jose Reis
148-149	Aloysius Niabu	North Solomons	Jose Reis	Jose Reis
150-151	James Muli	Southern Highlands	Jose Reis	Jose Reis/ Samson Tatakali
152-153	Akapina Tonave	East Sepik	Jose Reis	Jose Reis
154-155	Angela Soso	Eastern Highlands	Jose Reis	Jose Reis
156-157	Gladys Yadiwillo	Eastern Highlands	Jose Reis	Jose Reis
157-158	Leo Tohichem	Eastern Highlands	Jose Reis	Jose Reis
159-161	Wariopa Kenda	Eastern Highlands	Jose Reis	Jose Reis
160-161	Niki Amaia	Eastern Highlands	Jose Reis	Jose Reis
162	Labai Toani	National Capital	Eisuke Shimauchi	Tapei Martin
164-165	Timothy Kilami	National Capital	Eisuke Shimauchi	Tapei Martin
166	Alembo Nano	National Capital	Eisuke Shimauchi	Tapei Martin
167	Sister Balbine	National Capital	Eisuke Shimauchi	Tapei Martin
168-169	Ruki Fame	National Capital	Jose Reis	Jose Reis
170-173	Boroko Youth	National Capital	Jose Reis	Steven Mago
174-174	Henry Miro & Torua	National Capital	Jose Reis	Elton Brash
178-179	Weni Moka	National Capital	Eisuke Shimauchi	Patrick Matbob
180-181	Paulus Kombo	Melbourne	Dave Peterson	Dave Peterson
182	Gordon Gaius	East New Britain	Jose Reis	Jose Reis
183T	John Wong	East New Britain	Jose Reis	Jose Reis
183B	George Telek	East New Britain	Jose Reis	Jose Reis
184-185	Leonie Kanawi	Eastern Highlands	Jose Reis	Jose Reis
186-187	Regina Tulsa	North Solomons	Jose Reis	Jose Reis
188-189	Albert Toro	North Solomons	Jose Reis	Jose Reis
190-191	Anita Toro	North Solomons	Jose Reis	Jose Reis
192T	Ru Kundil	Western Highlands	Jose Reis	Jose Reis/ Joseph Ketan
192M	Sir Wamp Wan	Western Highlands	Jose Reis	Jose Reis/ Maggie Wilson
192B	Peter Peraki	Enga	Eosilo Shimauchi	Samson Chicki
193T	Peter Kama Kerpi	Simbu	Jose Reis	Jose Reis
193M	Auwo Ketauwo	Eastern Highlands	Jose Reis	Jose Reis
193B	Edward Piawe	Southern Highlands	Jose Reis	Jose Reis
194T	Lahui Tau	National Capital	Eisuke Shimauchi	Patrick Matbob
194B	Henry Moses	North Solomons	Jose Reis	Jose Reis
195T	Angela Soso	Eastern Highlands	Jose Reis	Jose Reis
195B	Patrick Itta	North Solomons	Jose Reis	Jose Reis
196T	Joseph Herman	Madang	Rocky Roe	Rocky Roe
196B	Gladys Yadiwillo	Eastern Highlands	Jose Reis	Jose Reis
197T	John Tieson	North Solomons	Jose Reis	Jose Reis
197B	Gabriel Koapi	East Sepik	Jose Reis	Jose Reis
198-201	Michael Somare	East Sepik	Jose Reis	Elton Brash
202	16 September 1985	National Capital	Jose Reis	

Legend: T = Top, M = Middle, B = Bottom, R = Right, C = Centre, L = Left.

Page No.	Name of Subject	Province	Photographer	Interviewer
120-123	Borok Pitalok	Western	Jose Reis	Chris Owen
124-125	Patrick Itta	North Solomons	Jose Reis	Jose Reis
126-127	Henry Moses	North Solomons	Jose Reis	Jose Reis
128-131	Gesengu Tangii	Southern Highlands	Jose Reis	Jose Reis/ Samson Tatakali
132-135	Peter Kankonaru	Morobe	Eisuke Shimauchi	Patrick Matbob
136-139	Benjamin Talai	East New Britain	Jose Reis	Jose Reis
140-141	Jerry Singirok	West Sepik	Jose Reis	Jose Reis
142-143	Jim Yer	Simbu	Jose Reis	Jose Reis
144-145	Toka Daina Yer	Simbu	Jose Reis	Jose Reis
146	Ruth Saovana-Spriggs	North Solomons	Jose Reis	Jose Reis
147	Rachel Kaetavara	North Solomons	Jose Reis	Jose Reis
148-149	Aloysius Niabu	North Solomons	Jose Reis	Jose Reis
150-151	James Muli	Southern Highlands	Jose Reis	Jose Reis/ Samson Tatakali
152-153	Akapina Tonave	East Sepik	Jose Reis	Jose Reis
154-155	Angela Soso	Eastern Highlands	Jose Reis	Jose Reis
156-157	Gladys Yadiwillo	Eastern Highlands	Jose Reis	Jose Reis
157-158	Leo Tohichem	Eastern Highlands	Jose Reis	Jose Reis
159-161	Wariopa Kenda	Eastern Highlands	Jose Reis	Jose Reis
160-161	Niki Amaia	Eastern Highlands	Jose Reis	Jose Reis
162	Labai Toani	National Capital	Eisuke Shimauchi	Tapei Martin
164-165	Timothy Kilami	National Capital	Eisuke Shimauchi	Tapei Martin
166	Alembo Nano	National Capital	Eisuke Shimauchi	Tapei Martin
167	Sister Balbine	National Capital	Eisuke Shimauchi	Tapei Martin
168-169	Ruki Fame	National Capital	Jose Reis	Jose Reis
170-173	Boroko Youth	National Capital	Jose Reis	Steven Mago
174-174	Henry Miro & Torua	National Capital	Jose Reis	Elton Brash
178-179	Weni Moka	National Capital	Eisuke Shimauchi	Patrick Matbob
180-181	Paulus Kombo	Melbourne	Dave Peterson	Dave Peterson
182	Gordon Gaius	East New Britain	Jose Reis	Jose Reis
183T	John Wong	East New Britain	Jose Reis	Jose Reis
183B	George Telek	East New Britain	Jose Reis	Jose Reis
184-185	Leonie Kanawi	Eastern Highlands	Jose Reis	Jose Reis
186-187	Regina Tulsa	North Solomons	Jose Reis	Jose Reis
188-189	Albert Toro	North Solomons	Jose Reis	Jose Reis
190-191	Anita Toro	North Solomons	Jose Reis	Jose Reis
192T	Ru Kundil	Western Highlands	Jose Reis	Jose Reis/ Joseph Ketan
192M	Sir Wamp Wan	Western Highlands	Jose Reis	Jose Reis/ Maggie Wilson
192B	Peter Peraki	Enga	Eosilo Shimauchi	Samson Chicki
193T	Peter Kama Kerpi	Simbu	Jose Reis	Jose Reis
193M	Auwo Ketauwo	Eastern Highlands	Jose Reis	Jose Reis
193B	Edward Piawe	Southern Highlands	Jose Reis	Jose Reis
194T	Lahui Tau	National Capital	Eisuke Shimauchi	Patrick Matbob
194B	Henry Moses	North Solomons	Jose Reis	Jose Reis
195T	Angela Soso	Eastern Highlands	Jose Reis	Jose Reis
195B	Patrick Itta	North Solomons	Jose Reis	Jose Reis
196T	Joseph Herman	Madang	Rocky Roe	Rocky Roe
196B	Gladys Yadiwillo	Eastern Highlands	Jose Reis	Jose Reis
197T	John Tieson	North Solomons	Jose Reis	Jose Reis
197B	Gabriel Koapi	East Sepik	Jose Reis	Jose Reis
198-201	Michael Somare	East Sepik	Jose Reis	Elton Brash
202	16 September 1985	National Capital	Jose Reis	

Legend: T = Top, M = Middle, B = Bottom, R = Right, C = Centre, L = Left.

GLOSSARY

Dokta Boi	Male nurse or medical orderly.
Haus Tambaran	Large sacred house used by men for traditional ceremonies and relics.
Kaukau	Sweet potatoes.
Kiap	Term used for Government patrol officers in the pre-independence colonial era.
Kina	Standard unit of PNG currency comparable to the Australian dollar.
Kunai	A tropical grass used for thatching houses.
Kula	Ceremonial and trading cycle in the Trobriand Islands and Louisiade Archipelago.
Lap Lap	Traditional wrap-around loin cloth.
Luluai	Traditional Village Chief or Big Man. The term was also applied to men appointed by the colonial government as their agents.
Manuntin Paia	Erupting volcano.
Mi stap natin	Hanging around doing nothing. Unemployed. At a loose end.
Moka	Traditional exchange for settlement of disputes or payment of compensation.
Mumu	A feast or way of cooking food in a pit.
Painim Wok	Looking for a job, getting employment.
Pasindias	Literally "passengers", "hangers on" unemployed people who live off the earnings of their friends or relatives.
Pig Bel	An intestinal disorder caused by eating bad pork.
Skul Bilong Wokim Piksa	Literally "School for Making Pictures". A Training Centre at Goroka for film makers.
Tapa	Beaten bark cloth usually decorated with traditional designs.
Taro	A tuber of the lily family, staple food of all coastal and lowland PNG people.
Toea	Standard unit of PNG currency corresponding to Australian cent.
Tok Ples	Local vernacular language.
Tultul	Australian Administration to represent the Kiap in the village.
Wantok	Literally "one talk" — someone who speaks your language. The term is usually used by people who have left their home village and recognise their affinity with fellow tribesmen who are similarly isolated.
Yanpela Didiman	Junior Agricultural Officer.